Feb 2010. Afghanistan

Alexs,
May this help you on your long journey,
to every Persian corner.
Travel well in the USSR,
Matthew

TAJIK-ENGLISH ENGLISH-TAJIK

DICTIONARY AND PHRASEBOOK

TAJIK-ENGLISH
ENGLISH-TAJIK
DICTIONARY AND PHRASEBOOK

JOSEPH F. CONROY
AND
FIRDAUS SHUKUROV

HIPPOCRENE BOOKS
New York

For information, address:
Hippocrene Books, Inc.
171 Madison Avenue
New York, NY 10016

ISBN 0-7818-0662-3

Printed in the United States of America.

CONTENTS

FOREWORD

I came to this project after two decades of work in Central Asian languages. As an undergraduate, I studied Classical Arabic for several semesters. This gave me confidence in reading and using the Arabic alphabet. In graduate school, I studied Farsi, the national language of Iran. Farsi is written in the Arabic script, but is an Indo-European language with connections, albeit tenuous, to English. My plans for a stay in Tehran were interrupted by the rise to power of the Ayatollah Khomeini.

Esperanto, the International Language, has been one of my working languages since university. Through it, I have done work in Breton and Basque. It was through Esperanto that I met my colleague in this current undertaking, Firdaus Shukurov, a native speaker of Tajik. At first, we conversed in Esperanto, but I soon learned that I could understand a good deal of Tajik from my experience with Farsi. We decided that it might be interesting to create a small dictionary and phrasebook for Tajik. This current work is the result of our efforts.

Firdaus Shukurov lives in Dushanbe, the capital of Tajikistan. I live on the east coast of the United States. Eleven time zones separate us, as well as many thousands of miles. Given the current situation in Tajikistan, the mail service is not the best. Fortunately, Mr. Shukurov has access to the Internet, so we worked together using e-mail. Since Mr. Shukurov does not know English, we used Esperanto as our bridge language. I set out phrases in Esperanto and sent them to Dushanbe. Mr. Shukurov wrote the Tajik equivalents to these sentences and e-mailed them back to me. I then provided the English translations for the Tajik sentences. In this way, we have endeavored to give you accurate Tajik expressions, presenting the language as it is currently used in Tajikistan.

Firdaus Shukurov and I both hope that you find this book useful and enjoyable. The Tajiks are a warm, friendly people with a long and interesting history. We look forward to sharing information about their language and culture with you. *Safaraton ba hayr bo mo!* Have a nice trip with us!

J.F. Conroy
April, 1998

THE TAJIK LANGUAGE

Marhamat ba zaboni tojiki! Welcome to the Tajik language! Tajik is the major language of Tajikistan in Central Asia. It is part of the West Iranian group of Indo-European languages, closely related to Persian (Farsi). The Iranian languages are distant relatives of English, but the relationship is so ancient that it will be of little help to the student of Tajik. About four million people speak Tajik in the Republic of Tajikistan as well as in bordering areas of Uzbekistan and Kyrgyzstan. It is also the language of the Jews of Samarkhand. Because of close contact, Tajik has been heavily influenced by the neighboring Turkic languages, much more so than Persian. Since Tajikistan was part of the former Soviet Union, the Tajik language has also borrowed heavily from Russian, especially in political, cultural and technical areas. Many of the abstract nouns in Tajik come from Arabic, much the same way as English uses Latin and Greek words.

The Arabic alphabet was used for Tajik until the early 1900s. This script was unsuitable for Tajik because it did not accurately indicate the vowel sounds. In 1928, the Roman alphabet was introduced and used until 1940, when the Cyrillic (Russian) alphabet was adopted. Beginning in 1994, the Tajikistan government instituted a project to return to the Roman alphabet. In this dictionary and phrasebook, we will use a Roman-alphabet version of Tajik, rather than the Cyrillic letters.

ALPHABET AND PRONUNCIATION

For this book we have devised a *transcription* of Tajik words into the familiar Roman alphabet used in English. A transcription is simpler to read than a *transliteration*, and our transcription follows the general guidelines of the Cyrillic-to-Roman project of the Tajikistan government.

The pronunciation of Tajik varies from region to region, both within and beyond the borders of Tajikistan. We have given the generally accepted pronunciations below.

The Alphabet:

The Tajik alphabet, in our transcription, consists of the following letters and digraphs (two letters representing one sound):

a b d e f g gh h i k kh l m n o p q r s sh t u v y z zh '

Since each of the alphabets used to write Tajik, the Arabic, the Cyrillic (Russian) and the English have a different alphabetical order, we have chosen one which is closest to English for convenience.

It is really not possible to convey the exact sounds of a language in print. What follows in an attempt to give the reader a rough guide to the sounds found in Tajik.

The vowels:

a	like "a" in *mat*
e	like "e" in *met*
i	like "ee" in *meet*
o	like "aw" in *saw*
u	like "oo" in *root*

Note: Where two (or more) vowels come together, be sure to give each vowel its own pronunciation. In *khonaam* ("my house"), for example, there are three syllables: *kho-na-am*. The letter **y** is used to form a diphthong, *ay*, which sounds like the **y** in English *my*.

<u>The consonants</u>:

The letters **b, d, f, g, k, l, m, n, p, s, t, y, z** are pronounced much as in English. The sound of **l** is always like that in *pull*, not like that in *milk*, and **s** is always as in *moss*, not as in *rose*.

The letters **gh, h, kh, q, r, sh, v, zh,** and **'** require some explanation.

The digraph **gh** represents a deep, French-style gargled **r**.

The Tajik *h*-sound is clearly pronounced in all positions: *hafta* ("week"), *fahmidan* ("to understand"), *roh* ("road").

We have transcribed the Cyrillic letter **X** by the digraph **kh**. This represents the sound of **ch** in German *Bach* or Scottish *loch*. For many Tajik speakers, **kh** sounds like a very strong *h*-sound. The word for "daughter," *dukhtar* may sound like *duhtar* for many people.

The letter **q** represents a *k*-sound made far back in the throat. To get a feel for this, compare the *k*- sounds in English *cook* and *kick*. The first sound is close to that of **q**. Some Tajik speakers pronounce both **k** and **q** the same, while others tend to swallow **q**, making it a gargling sound.

The letter **r** represents a trilled *r*-sound, like that in Spanish or Italian.

Sh has the same sound as in English: *shud* ("became") sounds much like English *should*.

The letter **v** has the same sound as its English counterpart, but for some speakers it may be closer to **w**, so that *vay* ("he/she") may be heard as either "vay" or "way," that is, like the English words *vie* or *why*.

Zh has the sound of English **z** in *azure*, or English **s** in *pleasure*. It is the sound of French **j**.

Finally, the symbol **'** is used to mark a catch in the breath, as when **tt** is dropped from *bottle* in certain varieties of English: *bo'le*.

A BRIEF SKETCH OF TAJIK GRAMMAR

It is beyond the scope of this work to present a complete analysis of Tajik grammar. What follows is a series of general comments on various aspects of the language. There are, of course, many specifics and exceptions which we will not have the space to explore. We have chosen the most important points of grammar for a beginner in the language.

Tajik recognizes the parts of speech familiar to English speakers: nouns, verbs, adjectives, adverbs, prepositions, pronouns and interjections.

Tajik nouns do not have gender; the same pronouns, *u* or *vay*, may refer to males, females, or objects. The plural suffix is *-ho* (sounds like English "haw"): *non*, "bread," plural *nonho*.

For specific direct objects, the suffix *-ro* (sounds like English "raw") occurs: *Man on kitobro doram*, "I have *that book*." This suffix is added last, after the plural suffix, and after any adjective: *Man on kitobhoi anglisiro doram* (mahn awn kee-tawb-haw-ee ahn-glee-see-raw daw-rahm), "I have those English books."

The suffix *-i* is used to express possession: *dusti Kosim*, "Kosim's friend/a friend of Kosim"; *manzili dusti Kosim*, "Kosim's friend's appartment."

Another suffix, also *-i*, is used to connect a noun with a following adjective. In Tajik, adjectives usually follow the noun: *rish*, "beard" + *siyoh*, "black" = *rishi siyoh*, "a black beard."

A third *-i* suffix is used to indicate an indefinite noun: *Kitobi doram*, "I have some book or other." Sometimes the number *yak*, "one," appears as an indefinite article. There is no definite article in Tajik.

As mentioned above, adjectives follow a noun which has the suffix *-i*:

shiri khub	good milk
moshini surk	a red car

The adjective suffix *-tar* is like the English ending "-er":

kutoh > *kutohtar*	short > shorter

The adjective suffix *-tarin* is like the English ending "-est":

kutoh > *kutohtarin*	short > shortest

The adjective *khub* ("good") is irregular:

khub	good
behtar	better
behtarin	best

Because Tajik verbs have endings to indicate which person is doing the action (much like Spanish), personal pronouns are often emphatic. These pronouns are:

I	*man*
we	*mo*
you	*shumo*
he, she, it	*vay* (*u*)
they	*onho*

Notes:

1. There is another pronoun for "you" with its own set of verb endings. This is *tu*; it is used as a *familiar* singular form. In the phrasebook, we have used the polite *shumo* almost exclusively, since this is the most useful form for a visitor to Tajikistan.

2. The choice of *vay* or *u* to refer to a third-person is a matter of preference. To some speakers, *u* does not convey a sufficient sense of respect.

These pronouns may be used after a noun with the possessive suffix *-i*:

dusti man	my friend
modari shumo	your mother

dukhtari vay	his/her daughter
khonai onho	their house

There are also *possessive suffixes* for the pronouns. Here are some examples:

dustam (*dust* + *-am*)	my friend
dustamon (*dust* + *-amon*)	our friend
dustaton (*dust* + *-aton*)	your friend
dustash (*dust* + *-ash*)	his/her friend

Indirect objects occur after the preposition *ba*:

ba man	to me
ba shumo	to you

Direct objects use the suffix *-ro*:

maro	me
moro	us
shumoro	you
vayro (*uro*)	him/her/it
onhoro	them

The infinitive in Tajik ends in either *-dan* or *-tan*: *fahmidan*, "to understand"; *doshtan*, "to have." To form the past tense, we use the *past stem* which is found by dropping the *-an* of the infinitive. To this we add the following endings:

I	*-am*
we	*-em*
you (familiar)	*-i*
you	*-ed*
he/she/it	*-Ø* (no ending)
they	*-and*

Here are the past forms for the two verbs given above:

fahmidam	*doshtam*
fahmidem	*doshtem*
fahmidi	*doshti*
fahmided	*doshted*
fahmid	*dosht*
fahmidand	*doshtand*

The past tense is the most regular form of the Tajik verb.

To form the present tense, we use the *present stem* which is found by dropping the *-dan/-tan* of the infinitive. Here are two examples:

infinitive	*khurdan* (to eat)	*tarsidan* (to fear)
past stem	*khurd-*	*tarsid-*
present stem	*khur-*	*tars-*

To the present stem we add the following endings:

I	*-am*
we	*-em*
you (familiar)	*-i*
you	*-ed*
he/she/it	*-ad*
they	*-and*

The present tense also uses the prefix *me-* for each form. This denotes on-going action. Here are the present-tense forms for the two verbs given above:

mekhuram	*metarsam*
mekhurem	*metarsem*
mekhuri	*metarsi*
mekhured	*metarsed*

mekhurad	*metarsad*
mekhurand	*metarsand*

There are many small irregularities in the present stems of Tajik verbs. Here is a short list to give you a feel for these forms. We list the infinitive, first-person past tense, first-person present tense.

to know a fact	*donistan*	*donistam*	*medonam*
to say	*guftan*	*guftam*	*meguyam*
to stand	*istodan*	*istodam*	*meistam*
to do	*kardan*	*kardam*	*mekunam*
to want	*khostan*	*khostam*	*mekhoham*
to write	*navishtan*	*navishtam*	*menavisam*
to come	*omadan*	*omadam*	*meoyam*
to study	*omukhtan*	*omukhtam*	*meomuzam*
to go	*raftan*	*raftam*	*meravam*
to drive	*rondan*	*rondam*	*meronam*
to know someone	*shinohtan*	*shinotam*	*meshinosam*
to become	*shostan*	*shudam*	*meshavam*
to hit	*zadan*	*zadam*	*mezanam*

To form the negative, the prefix *na-* is used. In the present tense, this prefix comes before the *me-*.

raftam, "I went"	> *naraftam*, "I didn't go"
meravam, "I am going"	> *nameravam*, "I am not going"

The verb "to have," *doshtan*, does not use the prefix *me-* in the present tense:

to have	*doshtan*	*doshtam*	*doram*
doram	I have		
dored	you have		
dorad	he/she/it has		

The verb "to see," *didan*, is not used in the present tense. Instead, the stem *bin-* occurs:

to see	*didan*	*didam*	*mebinam*
didand	they saw		
mebinand	they see		

The verb "to be" is *budan.* In the past tense, the forms are regular: *budam, budem, buded, bud, budand.* In the present tense, there are two sets of forms, one emphatic, the other normal. The forms are:

hastam, hastem, hasti, hasted, hast, hastand

The non-emphatic forms are:

am, em, i, ed, ast, and

These are found, for example, with the verb *istodan* and the *short infinitive* (minus the *-dan/-tan*) in a present progressive form:

man istodaam guft, "I am (right now) saying"

mo istodaem khur, "we are eating"

tu istodai khur, "you (familiar) are eating"

shumo istodaed fahmid, "you understand"

vay istodaast ron, "he/she is driving"

onho istodaand kar, "they are doing/making"

The negative of *ast* is *nest.*

To express the future, Tajik speakers often use the present tense. They may also use the verb *khostan* with the short infinitive. In this case, the prefix *me-* will not occur:

man khoham fahmid, "I shall understand"

mo khohem fahmid, "we shall understand"

tu khohi fahmid, "you (familiar) will understand"

shumo khohed fahmid, "you will understand"

vay khohad fahmid, "he/she will understand"

onho khohand fahmid, "they will understand"

One of the notable features of the Tajik verb system is the small number of verbs. To make up for this, Tajik makes wide use of *compound verbs*. One of the most frequently used forms in a compound is the verb *kardan*, "to make/do." Here are some examples:

gush kardan	- to listen
gush kardam	- I listened
gush mekunam	- I am listening
Man ba shumo gush mekunam	"I am listening to you."
Vay ba muziqi gush kard	"He listened to the music."
faromush kardan	- to forget
faromush karded	- you forgot
faromush mekuned	- you forget
Oyo shumo nomi onho faromush mekuned?	"Do you forget their name?"

The verb *shostan* ("become") also occurs, usually in a passive or intransitive sense:

faromush shostan	- to be forgotten
Nomi vay faromush meshavad	"His name will be forgotten."
Nomi vay faromush shud	"His name was forgotten."
kushoda shostan	- to be open
Dukon kushoda meshavad	"The store is open."
Dukon kushoda shud	"The store was open."

Finally, the compound verb *harf zadan*, "to speak," will be familiar to every student of Tajik. Literally, this verb means "to hit the letter."

Ba zaboni tojiki shumo harf mezaned?	"Do you speak Tajik?"

Word-order in Tajik sentences tends to be Subject-Object-Verb, that is, the verb usually comes last in a sentence. To say "that man knows my son," we must rearrange the words as "that man my son knows." "That man" is *on mard*, "my son" is *pisar-am*, and "knows" is *meshinosad*. The sentence will read:

On mard pisaram meshinosad.

In general, modifiers (adjectives, etc.) will follow the noun. To say "blue book," we begin with "book," *kitob*, add the connector *-i*, then use the adjective "blue," *kabud*: *kitobi kabud*.

Here are some further examples of Tajik syntax:

"I don't understand this word."

Man in kalimaro namefahmam.

Here, *man* is "I," *in kalima-ro* is "this word" as a specific object, and *na-me-fahm-am* is the verb, "I don't understand."

"My house is white."

Khonai man safod ast.

Here, *khona-i* is "house-of," *man* is "I," *safod* is "white" and *ast* is "is."

"Why are you not saying anything?"

Baroi chi shumo hech chiz nameguyed?

We have *baroi chi*, "why," *shumo*, "you," *hech chiz*, "anything," and *na-me-guy-ed*, "you are not saying."

"Today it will snow in the mountains."

Imruz dar kuhiston barf meborad.

Imruz is "today," *dar kuhiston* is "in the mountains, *barf me-bor-ad*, "snow will fall."

"I lost the key to my house."

Man kalidi khonaamro gum kardam.

Here we have *man*, "I," *kalid-i*, "key-of," *khona-am-ro*, "house-my (as specific object)," and *gum kard-am*, "I lost."

"This hen lays many eggs."

In murgh tukhumi bisyor mezoyad.

In murgh means "this hen," *tukhum* is "egg(s)" with the connective suffix *-i*, *bisyor* is "many," and *me-zoy-ad* is the verb "lays."

"The duck went to the lake with her ducklings."

Murghobi bo chujahoyash ba kul raft.

The word for "duck" is *murgh-obi*, "water-hen." *Bo* means "with." "Her ducklings" is *chuja*, "duckling," the plural suffix *-ho*, and the possessive suffix *-(y)ash*, "his/her/its." *Ba kul* means "to (the) lake," and *raft* is the verb "he/she went."

"My father has a long black beard."

Padari man rishi siyohi daroz dorad.

"My father" is *padar-i man*, "father-of-I." "Long black beard" is *rish-i siyoh-i daroz*, "beard-connector, black-connector, long." The verb is *dor-ad*, "he/she has."

TAJIK-ENGLISH DICTIONARY

Nouns are give in the singular form without suffixes. Verbs are given in the infinitive with the present stem indicated in parentheses. For compound verbs, both words are given.

A

abo	raincoat
abr	cloud
aeroport	airport
afsus	unfortunately
agar	if
aholi	inhabitant
ajoib	interesting
aka	brother
akhlotkutti	trash can
alakay	already
albatta	of course!
-am (suffix)	my
ama	aunt (father's sister)
amak	uncle (father's brother)
ammo	but
amriko	America
anglisi	English
angur	grapes
angusht	finger
anor	pomegranate
apa	sister
aparat	apparatus, appliance

aparati radio	radio set
apelsin	orange (fruit)
arobai ducharka	cart
arzon	inexpensive
asal	honey
asp	horse
-ash (suffix)	his, her its (suffix)
asrimiyonag(i)	medieval
assalomu-alaykum	peace be with you (a greeting—Arabic)
-aton (suffix)	your
Avghoniston	Afghanistan
avtobus	bus
az	from, about

B

ba	to
babr	lion
bacha	boy
bad	bad
badan	body
bahor	spring (season)
bakhsidan	to excuse, pardon
baland	high
bale	yes
band	rope
bandak	string
barf	snow
ba rohat	comfortable
baroi chi	why

baroi on	because
baromadan	to leave
baromadgoh	an exit
barq	lightning
basta	closed
be	without
behtar	better
behtarin	best
bin (infinitive: didan)	to see
bini	nose
birinj	rice
bisyor	very, a lot, much
bluzka	blouse
bo	with, by (means of)
bobo	grandfather
bogh	garden
bolgha	hammer
borkhalta	backpack
boron	rain
bosakhovat	generous
boz	still
bozor	marketplace
bubakhshed	excuse me
budan	to be
bulka	(bread) roll
buqa	bull
burj	tower
buron	storm
buvi	grandmother

C

chana	sleigh
chand	how much/many?
changol	fork
chap	left (side)
chaqra	a drop
charogh	lamp
chasm	eye
chatr	umbrella
cheki bank	bank check
cheki sayru sayohat	traveler's check
chi	what
chi guna	what kind of
chi hel	how
chi qadar	how much
chi tavr	how
chiz	thing
choy	tea
choykhona	tea-house
chuja	duckling
chunki	because

D

daftar	notebook
dahon	mouth
dandon	tooth
dandonsoz	dentist
daqiqa	a minute
dar	in
dar bolo	above, upstairs
dar boroi	about, concerning

dar nazdi	in front of
dar peshi	next to
dar	door
darakht	tree
dard	pain, ache
dard kardan	to hurt
dardi sar	headache
daromadgoh	an entrance
daroz	long
dars	lesson
dast	arm
dastak	glove
dastshuyak	a sink
der	late
devor	wall
didan	to see
(to) didana	goodbye
digar	(an)other
dina	yesterday
diqqat	attention
diqqat kardan	to pay attention
divan	sofa
domod	son-in-law
donish	knowledge
donishgoh	university
donistan (don-)	to know
dorusoz	pharmacist
doshtan (dor-)	to have
dugona	(female) friend
dukhova	oven
dukhtar	girl

dukon	store, shop
dungi	basket
dur	away, distant
durugh	a lie
dush	a shower
dust	friend
duyum	second (2nd)

E

ehtimol	perhaps
emon	imam (religious leader)
Eron	Iran
ezor	underwear

F

fahmidan (fahm-)	to understand
fardo	tomorrow
faromush	forget, forgetting
faromush kardan	to forget
farsh	floor
farzand	child
fasl	season (of year)
fil	elephant
firistondan (firist-)	to send
foram	beautiful
foridan (ba)	to be pleasing (to)
forsi	Persian (Farsi)
fransavi	French
furudgoh	airport
furugh	fortunate consequence

furukhtan (furukh-)	to sell
futbol	soccer

G

galstuk	a tie
garm	hot
gilem	carpet
gov	cow
gramatika	grammar
grip	the flu
guftan (guy-)	to say
gugird	a matchstick
gul	flower
gulob	rose
gum kardan	to lose
gumruk	customs (office)
gurba	cat
gurg	wolf
gurusna	hungry
gush	ear
gush kardan	to listen
gusht	meat

H

ha	yes
hafta	week
ham	also, together
hamma	every
hammomkhona	bathroom
hamqasb	colleague

hamsoya	neighbor
haq doshtan	to be entitled (to)
haqiqatan	in fact
harf	letter (alphabet)
harf zadan (zan-)	to speak ("hit the letter")
havo	wind, weather
hayvon	animal
hech	any; *used with negative:* no, none
hech chiz	nothing (with negative)
hech kas	no one (with negative)
hisob	(restaurant) check
hozir	now
Hudo	God
Hudo hofiz	God keep you!
hush	beautiful

I

iflos	dirty
iltimos	please
imkon doshtan	to be able
imruz	today
in	this, this one
injo	here (this place)
iroda	a desire
istgoh	(bus) station
istiqlol	independence
istiqomat	dwelling, residence
istiqomat kardan	to live (somewhere)
istodan	to stay, stand, be doing

J

jadval	ruler (for measuring)
jangal	forest
janob	sir
jarmarka	fair, market
jins	jeans
joi libosshui	laundry, laundromat
jomadon	suitcase
jorub	broom
juft	pair
jurob	socks, stockings

K

kabud	blue
kahva	coffee
kahvarang	brown
kalid	key
kalima	word
kalon	big
kalontar	bigger
kalontarin	biggest
kame	a little
kamzul	sportcoat, suitcoat
kamzulcha	vest
kardan (kon-)	to make, do
kartoshka	potato
kas	a person, one
kasal	ill
kasha	porridge
kay	when?

kelin	daughter-in-law
khalta	bag, sack
khargysh	rabbit
kharidan	to buy
kharidu-furush	business
kharita	map
khatarnok	danger
khele	very
khele ajoib!	Wow!
khesh	a relative
khirs	bear
Khitoi	China
khobkhona	bedroom
khojatkhona	restroom
khola	aunt (mother's sister)
khomushak	mosquito
khona	house
khonagi	domesticated
khondan	to read
khonum	lady
khor	thorn
khostan	to want
khub	good, well
khunuk	cold
khurdan	to eat
khurish	appetizer
khurok	food
khuroki peshin	lunch
khuroki shom	dinner
khurus	rooster

khushbakhtona	fortunately
ki	who
kift	shoulder
kishti	ship
kitob	book
konsulkhona	consulate
konvert	envelope
kor	work
kor kardan	to work
kord	a knife
korgar	a worker
korkhona	factory
kosa	a bowl
kuh	a mountain
kuhiston	mountains
kuhna	old
kujo	where?
kul	lake
kuloh	hat
kulula	round
kursi	chair
kurtai tag	shirt
kushoda meshavad	(it) is open
kutoh	short
kutohtar	shorter
kutohtarin	shortest
kvadrat	square

L

lift	elevator

lozim	necessary
lughat	dictionary
lukhtak	doll

M

mahkam meshavad	(it) is closed
mahqul	fine, acceptable
maktab	school
maktub	letter (to mail)
maktubi kushoda	postcard ("open letter")
majala	department store
malla	blond
mamlakat	land, country
man	I
-i man	of me: my
manzil	room, appartment
mard	man
mardona	masculine
marhamat	welcome
markaz	center
ba markazi shahr	in center city
maro	me
masjid	mosque
maslihat	advice
maslihat kardan	to give advice, suggest
masofat	distance
maviz	raisin
may	wine
mayda	small
maymun	monkey
mehmonkhona	hotel, living room

mekhrubon	goodhearted
mi	sentence-final question particle
mikrorayon	district
minnat	gratitude
minnat doshtan (dor-)	to thank ("have gratitude")
miz	table
mo	we
modar	mother
moh	month
mohi	fish
mohtob	moon
mor	snake
moro	us
moshin	car, auto
moshini borkash	truck
motoroller	motorscooter
motosikl	motorcycle
muallim	teacher (m.)
muallima	teacher (f.)
muassisa	office
muhandis	engineer
muloqot	meeting
murch	pepper (spice)
murcha	ant
murgh	hen
murghobi	duck ("water-hen")
murvattobak	screwdriver
mush	mouse
mushkil	difficult

mustahkam	strong
muzey	museum
muziqi	music

N

nabera	grandchild
naghz	well
naghz didan	to like to
nakhud	peas
namearzad	you're welcome
narkh	price
navishtan (navis-)	to write
navor	film, a movie
nazd	courtyard
ne	no
nigoh kardan	to look
nisf	one-half
nisfiruz	noon
nok	pear
nom	name
non	bread
nondonu	breadbasket
nonkhurak	cockroach
nonishta	breakfast
nonpaz	bread baker
nul	(bird's) beak
nuqragi	silver-colored
nur	a light
nushok	beverage
nushoki	drinkable

O

ob	water
obbozi	a bath
obi jav	beer
obu havo	weather ("water and wind")
oftob	sun
ohan	iron
oila	family
oilador	married
olu	plum
omad	arrival
omadan (oy-)	to come
omukhtan (omuz-)	to study
on	that, that person
onho	they
onhoro	them
onjo	there
orinj	elbow
oru	bee(s)
oshkhona	kitchen
osmon	the sky
osontarin	easiest
otash	a fire
oyo	introduces a question

P

padar	father
paket	package
panjai dast	hand

paranda	bird
pasha	a fly
pasport	passport
pero	pen
peshkhizmat	waiter
peshnihod kardan	to recommend
pisar	boy
pivo	beer
piyola	cup
plita	gas range, stove
poizd	a train
polis	police
polischi	policeman
poliskhona	police station
po(y)	foot
poyafzol	shoe
pukkashak	corkscrew
pul	money
pursidan	to ask
pushok	clothing
pusht	the back

Q

qaichi	scissors
qaiz	boat
qalam	pencil
qasr	palace
qator	train
qimat	expensive
qishloq	village

qishloqi	villager
qolin	carpet
qoshuq	spoon
qoz	goose
qudo	in-law (father or mother)
qulf	a lock

R

raftan (rav-)	to go
rang	color
rangi gulobi	pink
ravghan	oil
ravshan	bright
restoran	restaurant
rish	beard
rishtaroshak	razor
roh	road
(ba) rohat	comfortable
rohbar	guide
rondan (ron-)	to drive
rost	right (side)
ru(y)	face
rubl	ruble (currency)
ruchka	pen
rughat	list
rukhsat	holiday
rumolcha	handkerchief
Rusia	Russia
ruz	day
ruznoma	newspaper

S

sabr kardan	to wait
sabuk	lightweight
sabz	green
sachoq	napkin, towel
safar	trip
safed	white
saforatkhona	embassy
sag	dog
sala	turban
sanduq	box
sar	head
satil	bucket
savdo	commerce
savhamonak	record player
sayohat	travel, tourism
sayora	planet
sayr	a walk, visit
seb	apple
shab	night
shabaka	net
shaftolu	peach
shahr	city
shahrcha	small city
shakalot	chocolate
shakar	sugar
sham	candle
sharob	juice
shartnomae	contract
shavhar	husband
shavq	interest

shift	ceiling
shikor	hunting
shim	pants
shinohtan (shinos-)	to know someone
shir	milk
shirkat	office
shisha	bottle
shodan (shav-)	to become
shohi	silk
shom	evening
shosse	highway
shtat	state
shu'bai aloqa	post office
shurbo	soup
shumo	you
sinamo	movie theater
sitora	star
siyoh	black
soat	time, hour, watch
soati dasti	wristwatch
soatsoz	watchmaker
sol	year
soniya	a second
soqi po	leg
stakon	a glass
subh	morning
sukut	silence
surogha	address
surkh	red
suzanak	straight pin

T

taassuf	regret
tabaq	a plate
tabib	doctor, physician
tagho	uncle (mother's brother)
tak-tak kardan	to knock
takror	repetition
takror kardan	to repeat
taksi	taxi
talabidan	to desire
tamoman	really
tanur	oven
taqriban	approximately
taqsimicha	saucer
taraf	side
tarsidan (tars-)	to be afraid
(ba) tartib	in order
tashakkur	thanks
tasma	belt
tavallud	birth
tavallud shostan	to be born
tavr	manner
tayloq	calf
tayor meshavad	(he/she) is ready
tayora	ready
telefon	telephone
telefon kardan	to telephone someone
televizor	television set
telpak	cap
tezutund	spicy
tiloi	golden

tiramoh	autumn
tireza	window
tobiston	summer
tochtacha	shelf
tojiki	Tajik (language)
Tojikiston	Tajikistan
tor	web
torik	dark
toriktar	darker
toriktarin	darkest
tortanak	spider
toza	clean
tu	you (familiar)
tukhum	egg
tundar	thunder

U

u	he, she
-u	and (suffix)
uro	him, her
ustukhon	bone
ustukhonband	skeleton
utoq	a room
Uzbakiston	Uzbekistan

V

va	and
vanna	bathtub
vannakhona	bathroom
vaqt	time
az kadom vaqt	for how long

varaja	fever
varzish	sports
vay	that, he, she
vayro	him, her
vaznin	heavy
volidayn	parents
vazorat	ministry
viza	visa
vokzal	train station

Y

yakchand	several
yakh meshavad	(it) freezes
yakhdon	refrigerator
yakum	first
yelim	glue
yo	or
yubka	skirt

Z

zabon	tongue, language
zadan (zan-)	to hit
harf zadan	to speak
zamiston	winter
zan	woman
zanona	feminine
zard	yellow
zavod	factory
zebo	nice, beautiful
zhurnal	newspaper

zindagi kardan	to live
zonu	knee
zud-zud	often

ENGLISH-TAJIK DICTIONARY

A

(to be) able	imkon doshtan
about	dar boroi
above	dar bolo
ache	dard
address	surogha
advice	maslihat
to advise	maslihat kardan
Afghanistan	Avghoniston
(to be) afraid	tarsidan (tars-)
airport	furudgoh, aeroport
already	alakay
also	ham
America	Amriko
American	amrikoi
and	va, -u (suffix)
animal	hayvon
ant	murcha
appartment	manzil
appetizer	khurish
apple	seb
appliance	aparat
approximately	taqriban
arm	dast
arrival	omad
to arrive	omadan (oy-)
to ask	pursidan

attention	diqqat
aunt	khola (mother's sister); ama (father's sister)
autumn	tiramoh

B

back	pusht
backpack	borkhalta
bad	bad
bag	khalta
bank	bank
basket	dungi
bath	obbozi
bathroom	hammomkhona, vannakhona
bathtub	vanna
to be	budan
beak	nul
bear	khirs
beard	rish
beautiful	nebo, hush, foram
because	chunk, baroi on
to become	shodan (shav-)
bedroom	khobkhona
bee	oru
beer	obi jav, pivo
belt	tasma
best	behtarin
better	behtar
beverage	nushok

big	kalon
bird	paranda
birth	tavallud
black	siyoh
blond	malla
blouse	bluzka
blue	kabud
boat	qaiz
body	badan
bone	ustukhon
book	kitob
(to be) born	tavallud shostan
bottle	shisha
bowl	kosa
box	sanduq
boy	pisar, bacha
bread	non
bread baker	nonpaz
breadbasket	nondonu
breakfast	nonishta
bright	ravshan
broom	jorub
brother	aka
brown	kahvarang
bucket	satil
bull	buqa
bus	avtobus
business	kharidu-furush
but	ammo
to buy	kharidan

C

calf	tayloq
candle	sham
cap	telpak
car	moshin
carpet	gilem, qolin
cart	arobai ducharka
cat	gurba
ceiling	shift
center	markaz
center-city	ba markazi shahr
chair	kursi
check	hisob (restaurant); banki chek (bank)
child	farzand
China	Khitoi
chocolate	shakalot
city	shahr
clean	toza
closed	basta, mahkam
clothing	pushok
cloud	abr
coffee	kahva
cold	khunuk
colleague	hamqasb
color	rang
to come	omadan (oy-)
comfortable	ba rohat
commerce	savdo
consulate	konsulkhona
contract	shartnomae

country	mamlakat
courtyard	nazd
cow	gov
cup	piyola
customs (office)	gumruk

D

danger	khatarnok
dark	torik
daughter	dukhtar
daughter-in-law	kelin
day	ruz
dentist	dandonsoz
department store	majala
desire	iroda
to desire	talabidan
dictionary	lughat
difficult	mushkil
dinner	khuroki shom
dirty	iflos
distance	masofat
distant	dur
district	mikrorayon
to do	kardan (kon-)
doctor	tabib
dog	sag
doll	lukhtak
domesticated	khonagi
door	dar
drinkable	nushoki
to drive	rondan (ron-)

a drop	chaqra
duck	murghobi
duckling	chuja

E

ear	gush
easiest	osontarin
egg	tukhum
elbow	orinj
elephant	fil
elevator	lift
embassy	saforatkhona
engineer	muhandis
English	anglisi
(to be) entitled (to)	haq doshtan (haq dor-)
entrance	daromadgoh
envelope	konvert
evening	shom
everyone	hamma
to excuse	bachsidan
excuse me	bubahshed
exit	baromadgoh
expensive	qimat

F

face	ru(y)
fact: in fact	haqiqatan
factory	zavod, korkhona
fair (market)	jarmarka
family	oila
father	padar

father-in-law	qudo
feminine	zanona
fever	varaja
film (movie)	navor
fine	mahqul
finger	angusht
fire	otash
first	yukum
fish	mohi
floor	farsh
flower	gul
flu	grip
a fly	pasha
food	khurok
forest	jangal
to forget	faromush kardan
forgetting	faromush
fork	changol
fortunate consequence	furugh
fortunately	khushbakhtona
French	fransavi
friend	dust (m.); dugona (f.)
from	az
front: in front of	dar nazdi
to be frozen	yakh shodan (yakh shav-)

G

garden	bogh
girl	dukhtar
glove	dastak
glue	yelim

to go	raftan (rav-)
God	Hudo
good	khub
goodbye	to didana
goodhearted	mekhrubon
goose	qoz
grammar	gramatika
grandchild	nabera
grandfather	bobo
grandmother	buvi
grapes	angur
gratitude	minnat
green	sabz
guide	rohbar

H

hammer	bolgha
hand	panjai dast
handkerchief	rumolcha
hat	kuloh
he	u; vay
head	sar
heavy	vaznin
hen	murgh
her (possessive)	-ash (suffix); -i vay
her	uro; vayro
here	injo; dar injo
high	baland
highway	shosse
him	uro; vayro
his	-ash (suffix); -i vay

to hit	zadan (zan-)
holiday	rukhsat
honey	asal
horse	asp
hotel	mehmonkhona
how	chi hel; chi tavr
how much/many	chi qadar; chand
hungry	gurusna
hunting	shikor
husband	shavhar

I

I	man
iced	khunuk
ill	kasal
imam	emon
in	dar
in order	ba tartib
independence	istiqlol
interest	shavq
Iran	Eron
iron	ohan

J

jeans	jins
juice	sharob

K

key	kalid
kitchen	oshkhona
knee	zonu

knife	kord
to knock	tak-tak kardan
to know (someone)	shinohtan (shinos-)
to know (a fact)	donistan (don-)
knowledge	donish

L

lady	khonum
lake	kul
lamp	charogh
land	mamlakat
language	zabon
late	der
laundry	joi libosshui
to leave	baromadan (baroy-)
left (side)	chap
lesson	dars
letter (of alphabet)	harf
letter (to mail)	maktub
a light	nur
lightning	barq
lightweight	sabuk
to like to	naghz didan
lion	babr
to listen	gush kardan
a little bit	kame
to live (be alive)	zindagi kardan
to live (in a place)	istiqomat kardan
long	daroz

M

to make	kardon
man	mard
map	kharita
marketplace	bozor
married	oilador
masculine	mardona
matchstick	gugird
me	maro
meat	gusht
medieval	asrimiyonagi
meeting	muloqot
milk	shir
money	pul
monkey	maymun
month	moh
moon	mohtob
morning	subh
mosque	masjid
mosquito	khomushak
mother	modar
motorcycle	motosikl
motorscooter	motoroller
mountain	kuh
mountains	kuhiston
mouse	mush
mouth	dahon
movie	navor
movie theater	sinamo

museum	muzey
music	muziqi
my	-am (suffix); -i man

N

napkin	sachoq
necessary	lozim
neighbor	hamsoya
net	shabaka
newspaper	zhurnal, ruznoma
next to	dar peshi
nice	zebo
night	shab
no	ne
no, none	hech (with negative)
no one	hech kas (with negative)
nose	bini
notebook	daftar
nothing	hech chiz (with negative)

O

of course	albatta
office	shirkat, muassisa
oil	ravghan
old	kuhna
one-half	nisf
open	kushoda
or	yo
orange	apelsin
oven	tanur

P

package	paket
pair	juft
palace	qasr
pants	shim
parents	volidayn
passport	pasport
to pay attention	diqqat kardan
pear	nok
peas	nakhud
pen	ruchka, pero
pencil	qalam
pepper (spice)	murch
perhaps	ehtimol
Persian (language)	forsi
person	kas
pharmacist	dorusoz
pin	suzanak
pink	rangi golubi
planet	sayora
plate	tabaq
please	iltimos
to be pleasing (to)	foridan (ba)
plum	olu
police	polis
policeman	polischi
police station	poliskhona
porridge	kasha
postcard	maktubi kushoda
post office	shu'bai aloqa

potato	kartoshka
price	narkh

R

rabbit	khargysh
radio set	aparati radio
rain	boron
raincoat	abo
razor	rishtaroshak
to read	khondan
really	tamoman
to recommend	peshnihod kardan
record player	savhamonak
red	surkh
refrigerator	yakhdon
regret	taassuf
to repeat	takror kardan
repetition	takror
restaurant	restoran
restroom	khojatkhona
rice	birinj
right (side)	rost
road	roh
room	manzil, utoq
rooster	khurus
rope	band
rose	gulob
round	kulula
ruble (currency)	rubl
ruler (for measuring)	jadval
Russia	Rusia

S

saucer	taqsimicha
school	maktab
scissors	qaichi
screwdriver	murvattobak
season	fasl
second (2nd)	duyum
a second	soniya
to see	didan (bin-)
to sell	furukhtan
to send	firistondan (firist-)
several	yakchand
she	u; vay
ship	kishti
shirt	kurtai tag
shoe	poyafzol
short	kutoh
shoulder	kuft
shower	dush
side	taraf
silence	sukut
silk	shohi
silver-colored	nuqragi
sir	janob
skeleton	ustukhonband
skirt	yubka
sky	osmon
sleigh	chana
small	mayda
snake	mor
snow	barf

soccer	futbol
socks	jurob
son	pisar
soup	shurbo
to speak	harf zadan (harf zan-)
spider	tortanak
spoon	qoshuq
sport coat	kamzul
sports	varzish
spring (season)	bahor
square	kvadrat
to stand	istodan
star	sitora
state	shtat
to stay	istodan
still	boz
stockings	jurob
store	dukon
storm	buron
string	bandak
strong	mustahkam
to study	omukhtan (omuz-)
sugar	shakar
suitcase	jomadon
suit coat	kamzul
summer	tobiston
sun	oftob

T

table	miz
Tajik	tojiki

Tajikistan	Tojikiston
taxi	taksi
tea	choy
tea-house	choykhona
teacher	muallim (m.); muallima (f.)
telephone	telefon
to telephone	telefon kardan
to thank	minnat doshtan
thanks	tashakkur
that	on
them	onhoro
their	-i onho
they	onho
thing	chiz
this	in
thorn	khor
thunder	tundar
a tie	galstuk
today	imruz
together	ham
tomorrow	fardo
tongue	zabon
train	poizd, qator
train station	vokzal
trash can	yakhlotkutti
travel	sayohat
traveler's check	cheki sayru sayohat
tree	darakht
trip	safar
truck	moshini borash

U

umbrella	chatr
uncle	amak (father's brother); tagho (mother's brother)
to understand	fahmidan (fahm-)
unfortunately	afsus
university	donishgoh
us	moro

V

vest	kamzulcha
village	qishloq
villager	qishloqi
visa	viza
visit	sayr

W

to wait	sabr kardan
waiter	peshkhizmat
walk	sayr
to want	khostan (khoh-)
watchmaker	soatsoz
water	ob
we	mo
weather	obu havo
welcome	marhamat
what	chi
what kind of	chi guna
when	kay
where	kujo, dar kujo

white	safed
who	ki
why	baroi chi
wind	havo
window	tireza
wine	may
with	bo
without	be
wolf	gurg
word	kalima
work	kor
to work	kor kardan
worker	korgar
wristwatch	soati dasti
to write	navishtan (navis-)

Y

yellow	zard
yes	bale, ha
yesterday	dina
you	shumo; tu (familiar)
your	-aton (suffix); -i shumo

TAJIK PHRASEBOOK

Contents

THE PHRASEBOOK

GREETINGS

Salomot

Peace be unto you!	**Assalomu-alaykum!**

Note: This greeting is Arabic, and is used by Muslims throughout the world.

Good morning!	**Subh ba hayr!**
Good day!	**Assalomu-alaykum! Ruz ba hayr!**
Good evening!	**Assalomu-alaykum! Shom ba hayr!**
Good night!	**Shabaton khush!**
Welcome!	**Marhamat namoed! / Hush omaded!**
Welcome to Tajikistan!	**Marhamat namoed ba Tojikiston!**
mister, sir	**Janob**

Note: The terms *aka* ("brother"), *amak/tagho* ("uncle") are also used when speaking to someone.

lady, Mrs., madam	**Khonum (apa, ama, khola)**

Note: The terms *apa* ("sister"), *ama/khola* ("aunt") are also used when speaking to someone.

miss, young lady	**Dukhtar**

Greetings, Mr. Smith.	**Assalomu-alaykum janobi Smit (akai Smit, amaki Smit).**
How are you?	**Ahvolaton chi tavr?**
Fine, thanks.	**Hamaash naghz.**
And you?	**Azoni hudaaton chi?**
Well enough, thanks.	**Tashakkur hamma naghz.**
So, how's everything?	**Korho chi hel?**
What's new?	**Navigari hast mi?**
Nothing.	**Ne.**
How is your family?	**Oilaaton chi tavr ast?**

Note: Oila-aton is "family" with the suffix *-aton*, "your."

Everyone is fine, thanks.	**Hamma khub hastaand, tashakkur.**
Goodbye!	**To didana!**
Have a nice trip!	**Safaraton ba hayr!**
God keep you!	**Hudo hofiz! / Panoaton ba hudo!**

MEETING PEOPLE
Shinisoí

What's your name?	**Nomi shumo chist?**
My name is Kosim.	**Nomi man Kosim ast.**
It's nice to meet you.	**Khele hursandam.**
The pleasure is mine.	**Man ham hursandam.**
Who is that?	**On kas ki meboshad?**
Who is...	**On ... ki hast?**
that man?	**mard**

that woman?	**zan**
that boy?	**pisar**
that girl?	**dukhtar**
That is...	**On kas ... meboshad.**
my husband.	**shavharam**
my wife.	**zanam**
my son.	**pisaram**
my daughter.	**dukhtaram**
my neighbor.	**hamsoyaam**
a villager.	**qishloqi**
Allow me to introduce...	**Shumoro bo ... shinos khoham kard.**
my husband.	**shavharam**
my wife.	**zanam**
my friend.	**dustam**
my woman friend.	**dugonaam**
my colleague.	**hamqasbam**
Do you know him/her?	**Shumo vayro meshinosed mi?**
Do you know them?	**Shumo onhoro meshinosed mi?**
Do you know Saidro?	**Shumo Saidro meshinosed mi?**
Yes, I know him.	**Ha, man uro meshinosam.**
Do you know Tahmina?	**Shumo Tahminaro meshinosed mi?**
No, I haven't met her.	**Ne man vayro nameshinosam.**
Whom do you know in Tajikistan?	**Shumo dar Tojikiston kiro meshinosed?**
Unfortunately, I know no one in your land.	**Afsus, ki yagon kasro dar mamlakati shumo nameshinosam.**

I know Mr. Tursunzoda.	**Man janobi Tursunzodaro meshinosam.**
I know Mrs. Kosimova.	**Man khonumi Kosimovaro meshinosam.**
Now I know you!	**Hozir man shumoro meshinosam.**
Do you know Mr. Kosimov's address?	**Shumo suroghai janobi Kosimovro medoned mi?**
Yes, I know it.	**Ha, man medonam.**
No, I don't know it.	**Ne, man namedonam.**
Do you know his/her address?	**Shumo suroghai vayro medoned mi?**

BASIC EXPRESSIONS FOR CONVERSATIONS

Kalimoti asosii baroi suhbatguzaroni

Yes.	**Ha.**
Yes, that's so.	**Ha, in tavr meboshad.**
No.	**Ne.**
No, that's not so.	**Ne, in tavr nest.**
Yes, you are correct.	**Ha, shumo rost meguyed.**
No, you are wrong.	**Ne, shumo hato mekuned.**
Please.	**Iltimos mekunam.**
Thank you.	**Tashakkur.**
You're welcome.	**Namearzad.**
I thank you.	**Ba shumo khele minnat doram.**
Thank you very much.	**Tashakkuri ziyed!**

Excuse me, please.	**Iltimos mekunam bubakhshed.**
Please repeat that.	**Iltimos, takror kuned.**
I'm sorry.	**Taassuf mehuram.**
Do you speak English?	**Shumo ba zaboni anglisi harf mezaned mi?**
Does anyone here speak English?	**Kase dar injo ba zaboni anglisi harf mezaned mi?**
I speak only Tajik.	**Man kame ba zaboni tojiki harf mezanam.**
Can you speak...	**Shumo ba zaboni ... harf mezaned mi?**
Tajik?	**tojiki**
English?	**anglisi**
French?	**fransavi**
Farsi (Persian)?	**forsi**
Uzbek?	**uzbeki**
Esperanto?	**Esperanti**
Yes, a little.	**Ha, kame.**
Excuse me, I don't understand you.	**Bubakhshed, man shumoro nafahmidam.**
I know English, but not well.	**Man anglisi mefahmam, ammo naghz ne.**
I am learning Tajik.	**Man zaboni tojikiro meomuzam.**
Do you understand me?	**Shumo maro mefahmed mi?**
Yes, I understand you.	**Ha, man shumoro mefahmam.**
Alas! I don't understand you at all!	**Sad afsus! Shumoro namefahmam.**

Your language is beautiful, but difficult.	**Zaboni shumo khele hush ast, ammo mushkil.**
Let's speak Tajik!	**Bijoed ba zaboni tojiki harf mezanem.**

HOW DO YOU SAY...?
Chi hel boyad guft?

How do you say "book" in Tajik?	**Chi hel boyad guft "book" tojiki?**
You say "kitob."	**"Kitob" meguyand.**

Note: Tajik prefers the third-person plural for such general statements. *Me-guy-and* means "they say."

How do you say "hofiz" in English?	**Chi hel boyad guft "hofiz" anglisi?**
You say...	**Meguyand...**
What does "modar" mean?	**Kalimai "modar" chi ma'no dorad?**
"Modar" means	**Ma'noi modar "mother" meboshad.**
Does "devor" mean "house"?	**Oyo, ma'noi kalimai "devor" "house" meboshad mi?**

Note: Oyo introduces a question. The sentence-final *mi* also acts as a spoken queston mark.

No, "devor" does not mean "house."	**Ne, ma'noi "devor" "house" nest.**

It means "wall."	**Ma'noyash "wall" meboshad.**
Please speak slowly.	**Iltimos mekunam ohista harf zaned.**
I don't understand this word.	**Man in kalimaro namefahmam.**
Please write it out.	**Iltimos mekunam onro navised.**
Oh no! I forget!	**Afsus! Man faromush kardam.**
It doesn't matter.	**Hech gap ne.**
Listen, I'll repeat.	**Gush kuned, man takror mekunam.**

QUESTION WORDS

Kalimahoi Savol

Who? (Who? plural)	**Ki? (Kiho?)**
Who is that man?	**Vay janob ki meboshad?**
Who is this man?	**In janob ki meboshad?**
This is my friend, Firuz.	**In kas dusti man Firuz ast.**
To whom?	**Ba ki?**
To whom were you speaking?	**Shumo ba ki gap zaded?**
Of whom? Whose?	**Az ki? Az oni ki?**
Whose book is that?	**Vay kitob az oni ki?**
Whose book is that?	**Vay kitobi ki?**
That is Rudaki's book.	**Vay kitobi Rudaki meboshad.**
Who has the book now?	**Hozir ki kitob dorad?**

Whom did you visit in the town?	**Dar qishloq shumo dar peshi ki buded?**
Which (one)?	**Dar borai chi? (Chi hel?)**
Which book is that?	**In kitob dar borai chi ast?**
That is my book about Tajik.	**Vay kitobi man dar borai zaboni tojiki.**
That is my Tajik dictionary.	**Vay lughati zaboni tojikii man ast.**
What color is your house?	**Khonai shumo chi hel rang dorad?**
My house is white.	**Khonai man safed ast.**
What color is your car?	**Moshini shumo chi hel rang dorad?**
It is black.	**On rangi siyoh dorad.**

Note: Literally, this sentence reads "that color-of black has."

What sport do you prefer.	**Ba shumo kadom namudi varzish ma'qul ast?**
I prefer soccer.	**Man futbolro naghz mebinam.**
What?	**Chi?**
What is that?	**Vay chi ast?**
What is this?	**In chi ast?**
What are you doing?	**Shumo chi mekuned?**
I am studying Tajik.	**Man zaboni tojikiro meomuzam.**
I am working.	**Man kor mekunam.**
What is he/she doing?	**Vay chi mekunad?**
He/she is playing tennis.	**Vay tenisbozi mekunad.**
What are they doing?	**Onho chi kor mekunand?**

They are singing.	**Onho surud mehonand.**
What shall we do?	**Mo chi kor kunem.**
Let's go for a walk in the city.	**Mo dar shahr sayr kunem.**
Let's eat!	**Biyoed avqot hurem.**
What are you talking about?	**Shumo dar borai chi harf mezaned?**
I am talking about my visit to Dushanbe.	**Man dar borai sayr ba Dushanbe harf mezanam.**
Where?	**Dar kujo?**
To where?	**Ba kujo?**
Where is the mosque?	**Masjid dar kujo ast?**
Is it in the town?	**Oyo on dar qishloq meboshad?**
It's right here.	**On dar injo ast.**
It's over there.	**On dar onjo ast.**
right	**rost**
left	**chap**
It's on the right.	**On dar tarafi rost ast.**
It's on the left.	**On dar tarafi chap ast.**
Where am I?	**Man dar kujo hastam?**
You're in Tajikistan!	**Shumo dar Tojikiston hasted!**
Where is he/she?	**Vay dar kujo ast?**
Where are they?	**Onho dar kujo hastand?**
Where are you?	**Shumo dar kujo hasted?**
Where are you going?	**Shumo dar kujo meravid? (Tu ba kujo meravi?)**

Note: Someone who is not Tajik, or who is a beginner in the language, should be very careful before using *tu.*

I'm going home.	**Man ba khonaam meravam.**
Who is going home?	**Ki ba khona meravad?**
We are. We're going there.	**Mo. Mo ba onjo meravem.**
Where are they going?	**Onho ba kujo meravand?**
They are going to a restaurant to eat some *palav*.	**Onho ba restoran meravand baroi khurdani oshi palav.**

Note: Palav, a combination of rice and vegetables, is as ubiquitous in Tajikistan as pizza is in the U.S.

Where is there a good hotel?	**Mehmonkhonai khub dar kujo ast?**
Where is there a good restaurant?	**Restorani khub dar kujo ast?**
Where is Customs?	**Gumruk dar kujo ast?**
Where is the American consulate?	**Konsulkhonai Amriko dar kujo ast?**
Where is the American/ British embassy?	**Saforatkhonai Amriko/ Britaniya dar kujo ast?**
Where is the train station?	**Vokzali rohi ohan dar kujo ast?**
Where is the bus station?	**Istgohi avtobus dar kujo ast?**
Where is the airport?	**Furudgoh/aeroport dar kujo ast?**
Where are my suitcases?	**Jomadonhoi man dar kujo hastand?**
Where is there water to drink?	**Obi nushoki dar kujo ast?**
There's water in the tavern.	**Ob dar choykhona ast.**

Note: A *choykhona* is literally a "tea-house." These are the preferred gathering spots for socializing. One of the most popular *choykhona* in Dushanbe is called *Rohat*, "comfort, comfortable."

They sell bottled water here.	**Ob dar shishaho dar injo furukhta shudaand.**
Where are you from?	**Shumo az kujo hasted?**
I am from Tajikistan.	**Man az Tojikiston hastam.**
I am from the United States.	**Man az Amriko hastam.**
I am from China.	**Man az Khitoi hastam.**
I am from Uzbekistan.	**Man az Uzbakiston hastam.**
I am from Iran.	**Man az Eron hastam.**
I am from Russia.	**Man az Rusia hastam.**
Where were you born?	**Shumo dar kujo tavallud shuded?**
I was born in Dushanbe.	**Man dar Dushanbe tavallud shudam.**
Where was he born?	**Vay dar kujo tavallud shudast?**
He was born in New York, but he lives in Dushanbe.	**Vay dar Nyu-York tavallud shudast, ammo dar Dushanbe zindagi mekunad.**
Where do you live?	**Shumo dar kujo itiqomat mekuned?**
I live in the mountains.	**Man dar kuhiston itiqomat mekunam.**
I live in a small town.	**Man dar qishloqi mayda istiqomat mekunam.**

Where do they live?	**Onho dar kujo istiqomat mekunand?**
They live in a big city.	**Onho dar shahri kalon istiqomat mekunand.**
They don't live in Dushanbe.	**Onho dar Dushanbe istiqomat namekunand.**
We also live in a big city.	**Mo ham dar shahri kalon istiqomat mekunem.**
We live in Dallas, in the American state of Texas.	**Mo dar Dalasi shtati Teksasi Amriko istiqomat mekunem.**
Where do people speak Tajik?	**Ba zaboni tojiki dar kujo gap mezanand?**
People speak Tajik in Tajikistan, Uzbekistan, Afghanistan and Iran.	**Ba zaboni tojiki dar Tojikiston, Uzbekiston, Avghoniston va Eron gap mezanand.**
What other languages do they speak in Tajijkistan?	**Boz ba kadom zabon dar Tojikiston gap mezanand?**
Uzbek, Russian, Kirghiz, Totori, Koreyai and Ghayra are spoken.	**Boz ba zabonhoi uzbeki, rusi, kirgizi, totori, koreyai va ghayra.**
Wow!	**Khele ajoib!**
When?	**Kay?**
When shall we have dinner?	**Kay khuroki shomro khurem?**
When is the fair?	**Jarmarka (bozor) kay meshavad?**
When does the train (bus) leave?	**Poizd (avtobus) kay meravad?**
When does the bus from Dushanbe arrive?	**Avtobus az Dushanbe kay meoyad?**

When do the stores open?	**Dukonho kay kushoda meshavand?**
When does the Ministry of Commerce close?	**Vazorati Savdo kay mahkam meshavad?**
When does the museum open?	**Kay muzey kushoda meshavad?**
When does water freeze?	**Ob kay yakh meshavad?**

Note: The syntax of Tajik differs from English. This sentence reads literally, "Water when ice becomes?"

When is the market day?	**Ruzi bozor dar qishloqi varzob kay meshavad?**
When do you like to go for a walk?	**Sayrugasht kardanro kay naghz mebined?**
When the weather is nice, then I like to go for a walk.	**Agar obu havo khub ast, sayrugasht kardanro naghz mebinam.**
How long have you been in Tajikistan?	**Az kadom vaqt shumo dar Tojikiston hasted?**
For just two days.	**Hamagi du ruz.**
For how long have you been learning Tajik?	**Az kay boz shumo zaboni tojikiro meomuzed?**
For several months already.	**Alakay yakchand moh.**
When will Said come home?	**Kay Said ba khona barmegardad?**
He will come home when he finishes his work.	**Vay korro ba anyom merasonad, baad ba khona barmegardad.**
When will you come?	**Shumo kay meoyed?**
I will come when I am ready.	**Vaqte, ki tayor meshavam, meoyam.**

What kind of...?	**Chi guna? (Chi hel?)**
What kind of man is he?	**Vay chi guna mard ast?**
He is generous.	**Vay bosakhovat ast.**
What kind of woman is she?	**Vay chi guna zan ast?**
She is goodhearted.	**Vay mekhrubon ast.**
What kind of town is that?	**Vay chi guna qishloq ast?**
That is a small, but interesting town.	**Vay qishloq mayda ammo ajoib ast.**
What kind of cup is this?	**In chi hel piyola ast?**
It is a very old cup.	**In piyola khele kuhna ast.**
What kind of cups are those?	**Vay piyolaho chi hel hastand?**
Those are porcelain cups.	**Vay piyolahoi chini hastand.**
What kind of chair is this?	**In kursi chi hel ast?**
This is a comfortable chair.	**In kursi ba rohat ast.**
What is it like?	**In chi guna ast?**
It's big.	**In kalon ast.**
It's small.	**In mayda ast.**
It's long.	**In daroz ast.**
It's short.	**In kutoh ast.**
It's good, very good.	**In khub, hatto khele khub ast.**
It's heavy.	**In vaznin ast.**
It's light in weight.	**In sabuk ast.**
It's expensive.	**In qimat ast.**
It's inexpensive.	**In arzon ast.**
In fact, it is far too expensive.	**Haqiqatan, in khele qimat ast.**

It's a bargain.	**In narkhi khub dorad.**
It's round.	**In kulula ast.**
It's square.	**In kvadrati ast.**
What kind of tower is that?	**Burj chi guna ast?**
It is high and old.	**Vay balandu kuhna ast.**
What is the mosque like?	**Masjid chi guna ast?**
It is medieval.	**Vay asrimiyonagi ast.**
How's the water?	**Ob chi guna ast?**
It's very cold!	**Vay bisyor khunuk ast!**
How?	**Chi hel?**
How shall we go to Kurgon-Tepa?	**Ba Kurghon-Tepa chi hel rafta metavonem?**
By bus.	**Bo avtobus.**
What's the easiest way for me to travel to Tashkent?	**Chi hel ba Toshkant bo rohi osontarin ravam?**
Go to the airport and take a plane.	**Ba furudgoh raved va bo tayora parvoz kuned.**
How well do you speak Tajik?	**Shumo ba zaboni tojiki chi hel gap mezaned?**
I can only speak it slowly!	**Man ohista gap zada metavonam.**
How does the bus go to Kurghon-Tepa?	**Avtobus ba Kurghon-Tepa bo kadom roh meravad?**
It goes across the mountains.	**Bo rohe, ki dar kuhiston meguzarad.**
How shall I send this telegram?	**Man chi hel telegramaro firistam?**
Just go to the post office.	**Ba shu'bai aloqa raved.**
How far?	**Chi qadar dur?**

How far away is the town?	**Qishloq chi qadar dur ast?**
About three kilometers.	**Taqriban se kilometr.**
How far away is Shakhrisyabz?	**Shakhrisyabz chi qadar dur ast?**
About 500 kilometers.	**Taqriban panjsad kilometr.**
How far is Tashkent from here?	**Az injo Toshkant chi qadar dur ast?**
You have about two left kilometers until Tashkent.	**To Toshkant boz taqriban du kilometr mond.**
By car, the distance is not great.	**Bo moshin in masofat dur nest.**
For how long will you be staying in Tajikistan?	**Chi qadar vaqt dar Tojikiston meisted?**
I will be here for two weeks.	**Man dar in jo dar muddati du hafta meistam.**
Why?	**Baroi chi?**
Because/ for that reason	**Baroi on/ ki/ chunki**
Why are you learning Tajik?	**Baroi chi shumo zaboni tojikiro meomuzed?**
Because the language interests me.	**Ba in zabon shavq doram.**
Because I want to do business in Tajikistan.	**Man mekhoham dar Tojikiston kharidu-furush kunam.**
Why are you afraid?	**Baroi chi shumo metarsed?**
I'm afraid because you are driving so fast!	**Baroi on metarsam, ki shumo moshinaro khele zud meroned!**
Why did you call me?	**Baroi chi shumo maro jegh zaded?**

I called you because I saw a mouse.	**Man shumoro jegh zadam, chunki mushro didam.**
Why didn't you give him the newspaper?	**Baroi chi shumo zhurnalro ba on kas nadoded?**
Because I haven't finished reading it yet.	**Chunki holo to okhirash nakhondam.**
Why did she give them money?	**Baroi chi vay ba onho pul dod?**
She gave them money because they did the work well.	**Vay ba onho pul dod, chunki onho khub kor kardaand.**
Why didn't he open the door?	**Baroi chi vay darro nakushod?**
He didn't open the door because he didn't have the key.	**Vay darro nakushod, chunki kalid nadosht.**
Why aren't you saying anything?	**Baroi chi shumo hech chiz nameguyed?**
I'm not saying anything because I don't speak Tajik very well.	**Man hech chiz nameguyam, chunki ba zaboni tojiki naghz gap namezanam.**
Why aren't they coming to visit us?	**Baroi chi onho ba peshi mo nameoyand?**
They aren't coming because they don't have the time.	**Onho nameoyand, chunki vaqti kholi nadorand.**
Why did you arrive late?	**Baroi chi shumo der omaded?**
I arrived late because I got lost.	**Man der omadam, chunki rohro gum kardam.**
Why aren't they eating?	**Baroi chi onho khurok namekhurand?**

They aren't eating because they aren't hungry.	**Onho namekhurand, chunki gurusna nestand.**

LIKES AND DISLIKES

Chizhoi naghz dida shuda

Do you like to...?	**Shumo ... naghz mebined mi?**
read?	**...khondanro...**
to play sports?	**...varzishro...**
to travel?	**...sayohatro...**
to study languages?	**...omukhtani zabonhoro...**
to speak with foreigners?	**...gap zadan bo shahsone khoriji...**
Do you think that...is interesting?	**Ba fikri shumo in... shavqovar hast mi?**
music	**...musiqi...**
travel	**...sayohat...**
Do you think that... are interesting?	**Ba fikri shumo in... shavqovar hastand mi?**
sports	**...varzishho...**
movies	**...navorho...**
Do you think that this food is good?	**Ba fikri shumo in khurok bo lazzat ast mi?**
Yes, of course!	**Ha, albatta!**
I really like this kind of food!	**Man in khurokro khele naghz mebinam.**
What don't you like?	**Shumo chizro naghz namebined?**

I don't like dirty rooms!	**Khonahoi iflosro naghz namebinam.**
Do you like sandwiches?	**Shumo sandvichro naghz mebined mi?**
No, I really don't like sandwiches.	**Na, sandvichro naghz namebinam.**

NUMBERS
Adadhoi asosi

1, 2, 3, 4, 5	**yak, du, se, chor, panj**
6, 7, 8	**shash, haft, hasht**
9, 10	**nuh, dah**
11, 12, 13	**yozdah, duvozdah, senzdah**
14, 15	**chordah, ponzdah**
16, 17, 18	**shonzdah, habdah, hayhdah**
19, 20	**nuhzdah, bist**
21, 22	**bistu yak, bistu du**

Note: The *-u* on *bist* is the suffix form of "and."

23, 24	**bistu se, bistu chor**
25	**bistu panj**
26, 27	**bistu shash, bistu haft**
28, 29	**bistu hasht, bistu nuh**
30, 40, 50, 60	**si, chil, panjoh, shast**

Note: Only the vowel distinguishes between "three," *se*, and "thirty," *si*.

70, 80, 90	**haftot, hashtot, navad**
100	**sad**
110 rubles	**sadu dah rubl**

(Currently, one Tajik ruble equals 7 Russian rubles.)

about 100	**taqriban sad**
more than 100	**az sad ziyod**
almost 100	**qarib sad**
200, 300, 400	**dusad, sesad, chorsad**
500, 600	**panjsad, shashsad**
700, 800	**haftsad, hashtsad**
900	**nuhsad**
256	**dusadu panjohu shash**
485	**chorsadu hashtodu panj**
731	**haftsadu siyu yak**
1,000	**hazor**
1,047	**hazoru chilu haft**
2,000, 3,000	**du hazor, se hazor**
5,000, 10,000	**panj hazor, dah hazor**
45,000	**chilu panj hazor**
95,582 rubles	**navadu panj hazoru panjsadu hashtodu du rubl**
one million	**yak milion**
one billion	**yak miliard**

ORDINAL NUMBERS

Shumorai tartibi

first	**yakum**
the first gentleman	**janobi yakum**
the first lady	**khonumi yakum**

the first lesson	**darsi yakum**
the first three days	**se ruzi avval**
second	**duyum**
You are first and I am second.	**Shumo yakum hasted va man duyum.**
third, fourth, fifth	**seyum, chorum, panjum**
sixth, seventh, eighth	**shashum, haftum, hashtum**
ninth, tenth	**nuhum, dahum**
eleventh, twelfth	**yozdahum, duvozdahum**
some fractions	**yakchand kasrho**
half	**isf**
third	**seyak**
fourth	**choryak**
three-fourths	**se choryak**

HOW MUCH? HOW MANY?

Chi qadar?

How much does this book cost?	**Narkhi in kitb chi qadar ast?**

Note: Literally, this sentence reads, "Price-of this book how much is?"

How much does a room cost for one night?	**Narkhi yak utoq baroi yak shab chi qadar ast?**
How much is that in American dollars?	**Chand dolari amrikoi mashavad?**
Do you have a less expensive room?	**Utoqi arzontar dored mi?**

How much did you pay for that?	**Shumo baroi in chi qadar pul doded?**
How many flowers did you buy?	**Shumo chi qadar gul kharided?**
How old is he?	**Vay chandsola ast?**
He is forty.	**Vay chilsola ast.**

Note: "How old" is *chand-sol-a*, literally "how-many-year." The answer begins with the number, e.g. *chil*, "forty," then adds *-sol-a*.

How old are you?	**Shumo chandsola hasted?**
I am forty-five.	**Man chilupanjsola hastam.**
Are you really eighteen?	**Oyo shumo haqiqatan hayhdahsola hasted mi?**
How much milk is left?	**Chi qadar shir mond?**
How many fingers are on one hand?	**Yak dast chand angusht dorad?**
How many glasses are in the cupboard?	**Dar jevon chand dona stakon ast?**
How many people are at the table?	**Chand kas ba sari miz nishastand?**
Many.	**Bisyor.**
There are many people in the house.	**Dar khona bisyor kas hastand.**
How many people live in Dushanbe?	**Aholii Dushanbe chi qadar ast?**

Note: Dushanbe is the capital of Tajikistan. Before the recent political upheavals, about 800,000 people lived in the city. Thousands left during the fighting, then came back when peace was declared. The current population is thought to be around 900,000.

How many people speak English here?	**Chand kas dar injo ba zaboni anglisi harf mezanad?**
No one.	**Hech kas.**
Nobody speaks English here.	**Hech kas injo ba zaboni anglisi harf namezanad.**
How many children do you have?	**Shumo chand farzand dored?**
We have two children.	**Mo du farzand dorem.**
How many months are in a year?	**Yak sol az chand moh iborat ast?**
There are twelve months.	**Az duvozdah.**
How many days are in a week?	**Yak hafta az chand ruz iborat ast?**
There are seven days.	**Az haft ruz.**
How many days were you in Dushanbe?	**Shumo dar muddati chand ruz dar Dushanbe budet?**
I was only there for five days.	**Hamagi panj ruz dar onjo budam.**
How many fish did Kosim catch?	**Kosim chandto mohi giriftast?**
He caught four or five.	**Vay chor jo panjto mohi giriftast.**

TIME
Soat

one o'clock	**yak soat**
at one o'clock	**dar davomi yak soat**

two o'clock	**du soat**
at two o'clock	**dar davomi du soat**
a minute	**daqiqa**
a second	**soniya**
a clock	**soat**
a wristwatch	**soati dasti**

Note: The word *soat*, from the Arabic *sa'at*, can mean "time, hour, watch, clock."

What time is it?	**Soat chand shud?**
It's six o'clock.	**Soat shash shud.**
It's two o'clock.	**Soat du shud.**
It's three o'clock.	**Soat se shud.**
It's four o'clock.	**Soat chor shud.**
We left at two-thirty.	**Mo dar soati duyu nim baromadem.**
We arrived at a quarter after three.	**Mo dar soati seyu choryak omadem.**
It's five after six.	**Panj daqiqa az shash guzasht.**
It's a quarter after six.	**Choryak az shash guzasht.**
It's six-thirty.	**Shashu nim shud.**
It's not eight o'clock yet.	**Holo hashtu nim nashud.**
It's only eight-fifteen.	**Nav hashtu choryak shud.**
It's twenty of seven.	**Bist daqiqa kam haft shud.**
It's a quarter after seven.	**Choryak kam haft shud.**
It's ten of seven.	**Dah daqiqa kam haft shud.**

At what time is dinner tonight?	**Khuroki shom in shab dar soati chand meshavad?**
At what time is breakfast?	**Dar soati chand nonishta mekunem?**
At what time will we have lunch?	**Dar soati chand khuroki peshinro mekhurem?**
dawn; sunrise	**subh; tului oftob**
We'll have breakfast at dawn.	**Dar subhidam mo nonishta mekunem.**
noon	**nisfi ruz** (*nisf*, "1/2", and *ruz*, "day")
At little after noon we'll have lunch.	**Kame baad az nisfi ruz mo lanch mekhurem.**
At two o'clock we'll go for a walk.	**Dar soat du mo ba sajrugasht mebaroyem.**
Fifteen minutes after noon.	**Choryak pesh az nisfi ruz.**
Ten minutes before noon.	**Dah daqiqa pesh az nisfi ruz.**
a little before noon	**kame pesh az nisfi ruz**
At six o'clock	**dar soati shash**
At seven we'll have dinner.	**Dar soati haft mo khuroki shom mekhurem.**
midnight	**nisfi shab**
thirty minutes after midnight	**nimta kam yaki shab / nimta baadi nisfi shab**
five minutes after midnight	**panj daqiqa baadi nisfi shab**
the afternoon	**baadi nisfi ruz**
morning	**subh / pagohi**
evening	**shom / begohi**

DAYS, MONTHS, HOLIDAYS
Ruzho, Mohho, Rukhsat

Sunday	**yakshanbe**
Monday, Tuesday	**dushanbe, seshanbe**
Wednesday, Thursday	**chorshanbe, panjshanbe**
Friday, Saturday	**jum'a, shanbe**

Note: The days of the week begin with *shanbe*, "Saturday." *Shanbe* means "market." The other days, except *jum'a*, prefix a number to *shanbe*. The capital city of Tajikistan had a traditionaly market-day on Monday, *dushanbe*, hence the city's name, *Dushanbe*. The word for "Friday," *jum'a*, is Arabic, and refers to the weekly Muslim day of "gathering" for prayers.

day, days	**ruz, ruzho**
night, nights	**shab, shabho**
The day is warm, but the night will be cold.	**Ruz garm ast, ammo shab khunuk ast.**
What day is it today, please?	**Iltimos, imruz kadom ruz ast?**
week	**hafta**
month, months	**moh, mohho**
four months	**chor moh** (no plural after number)
season	**fasl**
summer, fall	**tobiston, tiramoh**
winter, spring	**zamiston, bahor**
year	**sol**

Note: Two calendars are in use in Tajikistan: the Gregorian for business and civil affairs, and the lunar (Islamic) calendar for religious practices.

last year	**soli guzashta**
next year	**soli oyanda**
January, February, March	**yanvar, fevral, mart**
April, May, June	**aprel, may, iyun**
July, August, September	**iyul, avgust, sentyabr**
October, November, December	**oktyabr, noyabr, dekabr**
the first of May	**yakumi may**
the second of November	**duyumi noyabr**
the third of July	**seyumi iyul**
the seventeenth of March	**habdahumi mart**
What is today's date?	**Ta'rikhi imruz chi ast?**
It's the fifth of October.	**Imruz panjumi oktyabr ast.**
What date is today?	**Imruz kadom ruz ast?**
It's the fifth.	**Ruzi panjum ast.**
On the tenth, we'll be in Dushanbe.	**Ruzi dahum dar Dushanbe meshavem.**
In January the days are short.	**Dar mohi yanvar ruzho kutoh hastand.**
But in July the days are long.	**Ammo dar mohi iyul ruzho daroz hastand.**
On what date will you arrive?	**Dar kadom ruz shumo meoyed?**
I will arrive on the sixth of June.	**Man shashumi iyun meoyam.**
today, tomorrow, yesterday	**imruz, fardo, dina**
the day after tomorrow	**pasfardo**
the day before yesterday	**pariruz**
last night	**dina shab**
New Year's Day	**Idi soli nav**
holiday	**rukhsat**

Some Holidays in Tajikistan:

December 31 - January 1	New Year's Holiday
March 8	International Women's Day
March 21	Spring Holiday, *Navruz,* formerly new year's day
May 1	International Day of Workers' Solidarity
September 9	Tajik Independence Day
November 6	Constitution Day
Ramazan	the month of Ramadan, the most important holiday
Offering Festival	occurs in the month of *qurbon*, according to the Islamic calendar

WEATHER

Havo, Obu Havo

good weather	**havoi khub**
bad weather	**havoi bad**
rain	**boron**
snow	**barf**
wind	**bod / shamol**
sun	**oftob / khurshed**
cloud, clouds	**abr, abrho**
hot	**garm**
cold	**khunuk / sard**
cold weather	**havoi khunuk**
hot weather	**havoi garm**

The weather is good today.	**Imruz havo khub ast.**
The weather is bad.	**Havo bad ast.**
The weather will be bad.	**Havo bad meshavad.**
The weather was bad.	**Havo bad bud.**
The weather was bad all last week.	**Havo dar tamomi haftai guzashta bad bud.**
Yesterday the weather was wonderful!	**Dina havo bisyor khub bud!**
Fortunately, the weather will be good tomorrow as well.	**Khushbakhtona, fardo ham havo khub meshavad.**
How was the weather yesterday?	**Dina havo chi hel bud?**
How is the weather now?	**Hozir havo chi hel ast?**
What will the weather be like today?	**Imruz havo chi hel meshavad?**
What will the weather be like tomorrow?	**Fardo havo chi hel meshavad?**
It will be cold.	**Khunuk meshavad.**
It will be very cold.	**Bisyor khunuk meshavad.**
The weather will be very hot today.	**Imruz havo bisyor garm meshavad.**
Yesterday the weather wasn't cold.	**Dina havo khunuk nabud.**
Summer is hot.	**Tobiston garm ast.**
The sun often shines.	**Oftob zud-zud medurakhshad.**
Winter is very cold.	**Zamiston bisyor khunuk ast.**
There's often a freeze.	**Zud-zud khunuki mezanad.**

In the fall the weather is pleasant—not too hot, not too cold.	**Tiramoh havo khele khub ast - na garmu, na khunuk.**
Spring is beautiful.	**Bahor khele foram ast.**
Is the sun shining today?	**Oyo, oftob imruz baromad ast?**
Yes, today will be a sunny day.	**Ha, imruz ruzi puroftob ast.**
No, today will not be sunny.	**Ne, imruz oftob namebaroyad.**
Is the wind blowing today?	**Imruz shamol mevazad mi?**
Yes, in fact it's windy.	**Ha, sershamol ast.**
No, there's no wind today.	**Ne, imruz shamol nest.**
It will be windy soon.	**Ba nazdiki sershamol meshavad.**
Will it rain today?	**Imruz boron meborad mi?**
It's raining now.	**Hozir borida istoda ast.**
It's not raining now.	**Naborida istoda ast.**
It was raining before.	**Allakay borid.**
It's drizzling now.	**Kame borida istoda ast.**
It will rain tonight.	**In begoch meborad.**
Today will be a rainy day.	**Imruz ruzi boron ast.**
Will it snow tonight?	**Oyo, imshab barf meborad mi?**
Yes, I think it will snow.	**Ha, bovari doram, ki meborad.**
Look! It's snowing now.	**Nigoh kuned! Allakay borida istoda ast.**
It's snowing today in the mountains.	**Imruz dar kuhiston barf meborad.**
It was not sunny today in Dushanbe.	**Imruz dar Dushanbe ruzi oftob nabud.**

It's sunny today in Samarkand.	**Imruz dar Samarkand ruzi oftob ast.**
There's some fog this morning.	**Pagohi kame nizm paydo shud.**
It's not raining, just drizzling.	**Boroni sakht nest, ammo kame meborad.**
storm	**buron**
snowstorm	**buroni barfi**
There was a big snowstorm last week.	**Haftai guzashta buroni barfii hele sakht bud.**
The roads were blocked.	**Rohhoi moshin band budaand.**
thunder	**tundar**
lightning	**barq**
There was a lot of thunder and lightning last night.	**Shabi guzashta ra'du barqi sakht bud.**
Today is a cloudy day.	**Imruz abrnok ast.**
The clouds are very low.	**Abrho khele pastand.**
There's a beautiful cloud!	**Ana, abri zebo!**
the moon	**mohtob**
The moon is bright tonight.	**Imshab mohtob durakhshon ast.**
star, stars	**sitora, sitoraho**
The night is filled with stars.	**Imshab osmon pursitora ast.**
Which star is that red one?	**Vay sitorai surkh chi nom dorad?**
That's not a star.	**Vay sitora nest.**
Is that a UFO then?	**Oyo, vay ChNP ast?**

Note: **ChNP** stands for *chizi noma'lumi parvozkundanda.*

No, that's not a UFO!	**Ne, vay ChNP nest.**
That's a planet.	**Vay sayora ast.**
Which star is that big yellow one?	**Vay sitorai zardu kalon chi nom dorad?**
I really don't know.	**Man tamoman namedonam.**
Ask Nozim.	**Nozimro purs.**
the sky	**osmon**
Today the sky is a beautiful blue.	**Imruz osmon kabudzebo ast.**
The sky is usually blue when the weather is good.	**Odatan osmon kabud ast, agar havo sof boshad.**
It's midnight and the stars are bright.	**Nimi shab ast, va sitoraho medurakhshand.**
rainbow	**ranginkamon**
After the rain, one sometimes sees a rainbow.	**Ba'd az boron, ranginkamon yak chand bor dida meshavad.**
In the mountains, the weather is often bad.	**Dar kuhiston havo zud-zud bad meshavad.**
picnic	**sayri chaman**
If the weather is good, we can have a picnic.	**Agar havo khub shavad, mo metavonem sayri chaman tashkil kunem.**
the Zodiac	**burji duvozdahgona**

Note: Literally, *burji duvozdahgona* means "the twelve constellations."

constellation, constellations	**burj, burjho**

Ursa Major, Big Dipper	**Haft Dodaron**
the Pleiades	**zumra**
the constellation of Orion	**Burji Oriyon**
Leo	**Asad**
Northern Crown	**Toj**

Note: This word is of interest because *toj*, "crown," is the root from which *tojik*, "Tajik," and *Tojkiston*, "Tajikistan," are derived.

Libra	**Mizon**
Time always goes by so fast!	**Vaqt doim tez meguzarad.**
Yes, too fast, in fact.	**Ha, hatto bisyor tez.**

ARRIVAL IN TAJIKISTAN
Omad ba Tojikiston

airport	**furudgoh**
customs	**gumruk**
Do you have your passport, Sir?	**Ako, shumo pasport dored mi?**
Your passport, Sir?	**Pasporti shumo, ako?**
Yes, of course. Here's my passport.	**Ha, albatta. Ana pasporti man.**
And here is my visa.	**Va dar injo vizai man**
How long are you planning to stay in Tajikistan?	**Chi qadar vaqt shumo dar Tojikiston meisted?**
Two or three weeks.	**Du-se hafta.**
Will you be staying in Dushanbe?	**Oyo shumo dar Dushanbe meisted?**

For the most part, yes.	**Ha, qismi ziyod.**
But I intend to travel to some other cities.	**Ammo ba yak chand shahrhoi digar raftani hastam.**
Why have you come to Tajikistan?	**Baroi chi ba Tojikiston omaded?**
For business reasons.	**Bo sababhoi tijorati.**
Are these your suitcases?	**Oyo, in jomadonhoi shumo hastand?**
Yes. Two big ones, and this small one.	**Bale. Du kalonu in mayda.**
Do you want me to open the suitcases?	**Mekhohed ki jomadonhoro kushoyam?**
It's not necessary.	**Lozim nest.**
Good. Everything is in order.	**Khub. Hama ba tartib.**
You may now enter Tajikistan.	**Shumo huquq dored ba Tojikiston namoyed.**
How do I get to center city?	**Ba markazi shahr chi tavr rafta metavonam?**
There are taxis and busses in front of the airport.	**Dar nazdi furudgoh taksi va avtobus vujud hastand.**
How can I find a good hotel?	**Mehmonkhonai khubro chi hel yofta metavonam?**
Please go to the "Tajikistan" hotel. It is the best.	**Ba mehmonkhonai "Tojikiston" raved. Mehmonkhonai behtarin ast.**
How much does it cost to go to center city?	**Narkhi ba markazi shahr raftan chi qadar ast?**

AT THE HOTEL
Dar mehmonkhona

Good day, Sir. May I help you?	**Asalomu-alaykum, ako. Chi khizmat?**
I would like a room.	**Ba man utoq lozim ast.**
For how many people?	**Baroi chand kas?**
I am alone.	**Baroi khudam.**
For two people.	**Baroi du kas.**
For how many nights?	**Baroi chand shabonaruz?**
Let's say five nights.	**Hozira baro panj shabonaruz.**
Yes, I have a room.	**Ha, man utoq doram.**
Unfortunately, I don't have a room.	**Afsus ne, man utoq nadoram.**
May I see the room?	**Utoqro dida metavonam mi?**
Yes, this room is fine.	**Ha, in utoq mahqul ast.**
Unfortunately, the room is too small.	**Sad afsus, in utoq khele mayda ast.**
Do you have a bigger room?	**Shumo yagon utoqi kame kalontar dored mi?**
The room is dark.	**In utoq torik ast.**
How much is the room per night?	**Narkhi yak shabonaruz chi qadar ast?**
Is there a restaurant in the hotel?	**Dar mehmonkhona restoran ast mi?**
Is breakfast included in the price of the room?	**Narkhi khuroki nonishta ba narkhi utoq medaroyad mi?**

TELEPHONE AND MEETINGS

Telefon - Mulokotho

(on the phone) Hello!	**(ba vositai telefon) Asalomu-alaykum!**
My name is Mr. Smith.	**Nomi man janobi Smit ast.**
I have a meeting with the director, Mr. Rakhimzoda.	**Man bo direktor, janobi Rakhimzoda muloqot doram.**
I am calling for Mr. Muminov.	**Man ba janobi Muminov telefon mekunam.**
Is he in?	**Oyo, vay huzur dorad mi?**
Please tell him that I'll call back tomorrow?	**Iltimos ba vay guyed, ki man fardo boz telefon mekunam.**
Could you please tell me when he will be in the factory?	**Iltimos, guyed kay vay dar korkhona meshavad?**
I have the contracts he requested.	**Man on shartnomae, ki vay pursid doram.**
I am here on business, and would like to buy both finished goods and raw materials.	**Man bo tijorat mashghul hastam, va mekhoham molu ashiyoi khom kharam.**
I need cotton, cotton seed oil, aluminum, cement, and various kinds of cloth.	**Ba man pakhta, ravghani pakhta, aluminiy, cement va matohoi gunogun lozim ast.**
What kind of cotton do you need, regular or thin fiber?	**Ba shumo kadom na'vi pakhta lozim ast - safed yo mahinnah?**

Thin fiber, of course.	**Albatta mahinnah.**
How much are you selling it for?	**Narkhash chi qadar ast?**
For $100 a ton.	**Yak tona - sad dollari amrikoi.**
That's fine, Director. When can we draw up the contract?	**Khele khub, janobi direktor. Kay mo shartnomaro sohta metavonem?**
What is better for you? Money, or goods in exchange?	**Ba shumo chi behtar ast - pul yo mahsulot ba joi pul?**
How many plants are producing aluminum and cement?	**Chi qadar korkhonaho cementu aluminiy istehsol mekunand?**
We have a cement plant in Dushanbe and an aluminum plant in Tursun-zade.	**Mo korkhonai cementbarori dar Dushanbe va korkhonai aluminiy-barori dar Tursun-zoda dorem.**
How much does electricity cost in your country?	**Dar mamlakati shumo narkhi quvai barq chi qadar ast?**
Very little, but currently, because of high demand, we are not selling electricity.	**Khele arzon, ammo hozir az sababi zarurati ghojati, mo guvai barqro namefurushem.**
By what means are you planning to ship the goods to the border, by train or by truck?	**Shumo mahsulotro chi hel ba sarhad mebared - bo qator yo bo moshinai borkash?**
What kind of satin do you have?	**Shumo chi hel namudhoi atlas dored?**

Please show me some goods produced by the Tojikatlas company.	**Bemalol boshad, ba man gazvori istehsoli ittihodiyai "Tojikatlas"-ro nishon dihed.**
What kinds of cotton and silk goods do you have with national designs?	**Shumo chi hel matohoi pakhtagi va abreshimi nakshash milli dored?**
When will my order be filled?	**Suporishi man kay ijro meshavad?**
What kinds of local wines do you have?	**Shumo chi hel mayhoi mahalli dored?**

BRIEF EXPRESSIONS

Ifodahoi kutoh

If you are a beginner in Tajik, using a few of these expressions in a sentence will help you to sound more fluent than you are. Never underestimate the conversational value of a well-placed *ajib* ("well, now...") or *afsus* ("alas!").

also	**ham**
You, too?	**Oyo, shumo ham?**
Yes, me, too.	**Ha, man ham.**
Me neither.	**man ne**
thus, therefore	**inak / hamin tavr boshad**
a little bit	**kame**
a little bit more	**kame bisyortar**
well now	**kani / ajib / ha**
homeward bound	**ba khona**
at home	**dar khona**

in the countryside	**dar sahro**
in the mountains	**dar kuhiston**
by the way	**dar qavz**
alas!	**afsus / daregho**
only	**faqat / hamagi / ammo**
I have only thirty rubles.	**Man hamagi si rubl doram.**
Only I have thirty rubles.	**Faqat man si rubl doram.**
perhaps	**ehtimol**
it may be	**imkon ast**
one is not permitted.../ one cannot...	**kas ... imkon nadorad**
One is not permitted to go in there.	**Kas ba onjo raftan imkon nadorad.**
One cannot hear him.	**Kas vayro gush kardan imkon nadorad.**
One is not entitled to...	**kas haq nadorad**
One is not entitle to take anything.	**Kas haq nadorad chize girad.**
One is not permitted to sing.	**Kas haq nadorad surud khonad.**
One ought to...	**kas boyad**
One ought to keep quiet.	**Kas boyad khomushiro rioja kunad.**
One should knock before going in.	**Kas boyad pesh az daromadan darro tak-tak kunad.**
still	**boz / holo / hanuz**
Are you still hungry?	**Oyo, shumo holo gurusna hasted mi?**
at that time	**dar on vaqt**
Listen!	**Gush kun!**
Please listen!	**Gush kuned!**

Look!	**Nigoh kun!**
Don't look!	**Nigoh nakun!**
Please don't look!	**Nigoh nakuned!**
Take a look! (lit.: see!)	**Bin!**
Wait!	**Sabr kun!**
Wait for me!	**Manro intizor shav!**
Please don't wait for me!	**Iltimos, intizori man nashaved!**
Pay attention! Careful!	**Diqqat kun!**
Be quiet!	**Orom shav!**
Please remain silent.	**Iltimos mekunam, orom shaved.**
there (in that place)	**dar onjo**
very	**khele, bisyor**
very big	**bisyor kalon**
very good	**khele khub**
very well	**khele khub**
She sings very beautifully.	**Surudkhonii vay khele khush ast.**
already	**allakay / boz / qarib**
enough	**kifoya / bisyor / ba darajai kofi**
I have already eaten enough.	**Man allakay bisyor khurdam.**
too much	**az had ziyod / benihoyat**
Is the room big enough?	**Oyo, in utoq ba darajai kofi kalon ast mi?**
Well, as a matter of fact, the room is too small.	**Haqiqatan, in utoq khele mayda meboshad.**
again	**boz / az nav**
Please repeat [it] again.	**Iltimos, boz takror kuned.**
always	**hamesha / doim**

never	**hej goh / hej vaqt**
never before	**hej vaqt pesh**
somehow or other	**dar har hol**
often	**zud-zud**
soon	**ba nazdiki**
You will soon be speaking the language better than I!	**Ba nazdiki shumo zabonro az man behtar gap mezaned!**
suddenly	**nogoh / nogahon**
The train stopped suddenly.	**Qator nogahon istod.**
early	**peshtar / barvaqt**
The bus arrived early.	**Avtobus barvaqt omad**
something	**chize**
Look! There's something in the box!	**Bin! Chize dar sanduq ast.**
somewhere	**dar yagon jo**
He lives somewhere in the mountains.	**Vay dar yagon joi kuhiston istiqomat mekunad.**
sometime, ever	**dar yagon vaqt**
Have you ever visited Samarkand?	**Oyo, shumo yagon vaqt dar Samarkand budet mi?**
everything	**hamma chiz**
nothing	**hech chiz**
I understand nothing.	**Man hech chizro namefahmam.**
immediately	**hozir**
I'll follow your advice immediately.	**Man hozir maslihatatonro ba inobat megiram.**
without fail	**albatta**

You must learn some phrases without fail.	**Shumo albatta boyad yakchand ifodahoro az yod kuned.**
without doubt	**beshubha**
in this way	**in hel, in tavr**
Have courage!	**Daleriro!**
Bravo!	**Ofarini!**
See you soon!	**To ba qaribi!**
See you tomorrow!	**To pagoh!**
See you again!	**To didana!**
Farewell!	**Khayr!**

AT THE RESTAURANT: FOOD AND DRINK

Dar restoran: khurokho va nushokiho

food	**khurok**
mealtime	**vaqti khurok /soati khurok**
Come to the table!	**Ba nazdi miz biyoyed!**
Come, we invite you to eat with us!	**Biyoyed, mo shumoro ba khurokkhuri da'vat mekunem.**
Traditionally, our dinner consists of various dishes.	**Odatan khuroki shomi mo az taomhoi gunogun iborat ast.**
at the restaurant	**dar restoran**
I'd like a table for two.	**Miz baroi du kas mekhoham.**
I'd like a table for me and my colleagues.	**Man mizro baroi khudamu hamqasbhonam mekhoham.**

I prefer a table by the window.	**Man mizi nazdi tireza mekhoham.**
Don't you have a table somewhere else?	**Oyo yagon mizi digar nadored mi?**
We are too close to the kitchen here.	**Dar injo mo ba joi oshpazi bisyor nazdik hastem.**
Where is the restroom, please?	**Iltimos, khojatkhona dar kujo ast?**
Waiter! The menu, please.	**Peshkhizmat! Ruykhati khurokhoro biyored.**
What specialties do you have today?	**Imruz shumo chi khel khuroki hos dored?**
Which meal do you recommend?	**Kadom anvoi khurokhoro peshnihod mekuned?**
What would you suggest?	**Shumo chizro maslihat mekuned?**
I would like to have a local speciality.	**Man yagon taomi mahaliro khurdan mekhoham.**
Please bring me a glass of water.	**Iltimos, yak stakon ob ba man biyored.**
Please bring us tea and water.	**Iltimos, ba mo choy va ob biyored.**
a fork, forks	**changol, changolho**
There are no forks on the table.	**Dar boloi dastarkhon changolho nestand.**
Waiter, I don't have a fork.	**Peshkhizmat, man changol nadoram.**
a spoon, spoons	**qoshuq, qoshuqho**
We need another spoon.	**Ba mo qoshuqi digar lozim ast.**
a knife, knives	**kord, kordho**

Oh no! My knife fell on the floor.	**Sad afsus, kordi man ba farsh aftid.**
Please bring me another knife.	**Iltimos, yak kordi digar biyored.**
Please bring me a spoon and a fork.	**Iltimos mekunam, qoshuqu changolro ba man biyored.**
a cup, cups	**piyola, piyolaho**
a cup of coffee	**yak piyola kahva**
a cup of tea	**yak piyola choy**
Would you like a cup of coffee?	**Oyo, shumo ba yak piyola kahva mayl dored mi?**
Yes, very much.	**Ha, bo maylu raghbat.**
I would prefer a cup of tea.	**Yak piyola choyro avlotar mehostam.**
With sugar? With milk?	**Bo shakar? Bo shir?**
Without milk, please.	**Be shir, iltimos mekunam.**
a saucer, saucers	**taqsimicha, taqsimichaho**
Do you need a saucer?	**Ba shumo taqsimicha lozim mi?**
a glass, glasses	**stakon, stakonho**
a glass of water	**yak stakon ob**
a glass of beer	**yak stakon obi jav / pivo**
a plate, plates	**tabaq, tabaqho**
a bowl, bowls	**kosa, kosaho**
a bowl of soup	**yak kosa shurbo**
Two bowls of soup, please.	**Iltimos, du kosa shurbo biyored.**
a napkin, napkins	**sachoq, sachoqho**
a white napkin, white napkins	**sachoqi safed, sachoqhoi safed**

That napkin is dirty.	**On sachoq iflos ast.**
Is that napkin clean?	**Oyo, on sachok toza ast mi?**
No, it is not clean.	**Ne, vay toza nest.**
Take this one.	**Inro gired.**
Where is my napkin?	**Sachoqi man dar kujo ast?**
Waiter, please bring us a few napkins.	**Peshkhizmat, ba mo yakchand sachoq biyored.**
beverage	**nushoki**
Waiter! Come here, please.	**Peshhizmat! Iltimos, ba injo biyoyed.**
Do you have a wine list?	**Oyo, shumo ruyhati mayhoro dored mi?**

Note: In spite of Islamic restrictions on alcohol, wine and beer are available in Tajikistan.

Our wine list is small, but the wines are very good.	**Namudhoi mayho kamand, ammo mayho khele khub hastand.**
I would like...	**Man ... mekhoham.**
wine	**may / sharob**
red wine	**sharobi surkh**
white wine	**sharobi safed**
a bottle of water and four glasses	**yak shisha ob va chorta stakon**
Bring a bottle of soda, please.	**Iltimos, yak shisha obi soda biyored.**
mineral water	**obi madani'**
tea	**choy**
milk	**shir**

Tajik tea with butter and milk	**shirchoy**
kefir (a yoghurt drink)	**jurghot**
lemon soda	**limanod**
Orange Fanta	**fanta**
Coca Cola	**koka-kola**
appetizers	**khurishho**
What kinds of appetizers do you have?	**Shumo chi hel khurishho dored?**
We have *nishollo, sambusa*, and various salads.	**Mo nishollo, sambusa va salathoi gunogun dorem.**

Note: **Nishollo** is a sweet appetizer, made from egg whites and the roots of a local plant. **Sambusa** is a kind of small cake, made from dough, containing a meat and onion mixture or occasionally squash.

I'd like some soup. What kind of soup do you have?	**Man oshi suyuq mekhoham. Kadom namudi osh dored?**
We have *khomshurbo*.	**Mo khomshurbo dorem.**

Note: **Khomshurbo** is a soup of fresh meat, onion, potatoes, carrots, and turnips. By the way, *shurbo* comes from the Arabic *shariba*, "drink." The Arabic word was borrowed into Western languages as *sorbet* and *sherbet*, as well as *syrup*.

What do you suggest for our main course?	**Baroi khuroki asos shumo chi maslihat medihed?**

Note: Restaurants in Tajikistan prepare food in both Western and Asian styles. Some typical Tajik dishes are:

palav	oil, meat, onion, carrot, spices, peas, rice
sihkabob	grilled meat on skewers
gushtbiryon	meat, onion, spices
mantu	turnover stuffed with meat, onion, spices; a vegetarian version is made with squash instead of meat

What do you suggest for dessert?	**Baroi shiravori shumo chizro peshnihod mekuned?**
melon, watermelon, apple, pomegranate, grapes, raisins, and so on.	**tarbuzu harbuza, seb, anor, angur, maviz va ghayra**
Waiter! Please bring three Tajik-style teas!	**Peshkhizmat! Iltimos seto shirchoy biyored.**
Waiter! The check, please.	**Peshkhizmat! Iltimos, hisob kuned.**
meat	**gusht**

Note: Tajiks are fond of meat, and often use it in preparing dishes. To offer a guest a meatless meal would be considered an insult.

duck, beef, veal	**gushti murghobi, gushti gov, gushti tayloq**
venison, goat, chicken	**gushti gavazn, gushti buz, gushti murgh**
mutton, lamb	**gushti guspand, gushti barra**
fish, rabbit, steak	**mohi, khargush, bifshteks**

I prefer lamb to beef.	**Nisbat ba gushti gov man gushti guspandro naghz mebinam.**
Would you like to eat fish or steak?	**Oyo, shumo mohi mekhohed yo ki bifshteks?**
vegetables	**sabzavot**
cabbage, broccoli, onion	**karam, sarsabil, piyoz**
bean, string bean	**ghilofak, lubiyo**
cauliflower	**karami guli**
carrot, cucumber, squash	**sabzi, bodiring, kadu**
lettuce, corn, eggplant	**latuk, juvori, boimjon**
peas, potato	**nakhud, kartoshka**
tomato	**pamidor**
rice, turnip	**birinj, shalgham**
fruits	**mevaho**
apricot, cherry, lemon	**zardolu, olucha, limu**
orange, peach	**apelsin, shaftolu**

Note: What a long voyage **apelsin** has made! The orange was introduced into Europe from Asia via the Arabs, and the Germans called it *Apfelsine* ("Chinese apple"). The Russians borrowed this as *apelsin*, and the Tajiks, who live right near China, then acquired the word!

pear, apple, plum, grape	**nok, seb, olu, angur**
other foods	**khurokhoi digar**
bread, roll	**non, bulka**
butter, oil	**ravghani maska, ravghan**
salt, pepper	**ravghani dumba, murch**
porridge	**kasha**
egg, fried egg	**tukhum, tukhumbiryon**

juices	**sharobho**
orange juice	**sharobi apelsin**
apple juice	**sharobi seb**
coffee, tea	**kahva, choy**
hot chocolate	**shakaloti garm**
milk, iced tea	**shir, choi khunuk**
beer	**obi jav**
Which do you prefer, tea or coffee?	**Shumo chi mekhohed, choy yo kahva?**
Do you prefer potatoes or rice?	**Oyo shumo kartoshka yo ki birinjro mekhohed?**
I prefer rice.	**Man birinj mekhoham.**
Yuck! I hate peas!	**Ne! Man nakhudro naghz namebinam.**
But I really like spicy food!	**Ammo man khurokhoi tezutundro naghz mebinam.**

THE FAMILY
Oila

Are you married?	**Oyo shumo oilador hasted mi?**
No, I'm not married.	**Ne, oilador nestam.**
Do you have a wife?	**Shumo zan dored mi?**
Yes, I have a wife.	**Ha, man zan doram.**
Do you have a husband?	**Shumo shavhar dored mi?**
No, I don't have a husband.	**Ne, shavhar nadoram.**
Yes, I have a husband.	**Ha, man shavhar doram.**
Do you have children?	**Oyo shumo farzand dored mi?**

Yes, I have three children.	**Ha, man se farzand doram.**
Two sons and one daughter.	**Du pisar va yak dukhtar.**
father, dad	**padar, padarjon / ota, otajon / dada, dadajon**
mother, mom	**modar, modarjon / ocha, ochajon / oya, oyajon**
parents	**padaru modar / volidayn**

Note: The *-u* at the end of *padar* is the suffix form of "and."

My father lives in Dushanbe.	**Padari man dar Dushanbe istiqomat mekunad.**
My husband works in an office.	**Shavhar man dar muassisa kor mekunad.**
grandfather, grandmother	**bobo (padarkalon), buvi (modarkalon)**
grandparents	**boboyu buvi**
son, sons	**pisar, pisarho**
daughter, daughters	**dukhtar, dukhtarho**
His son is now in Berlin.	**Pisari vay hozir dar Berlin hast.**
Our daughter is studying at the university	**Dukhtaramon dar donishgoh mekhonad. ("-amon" = "our")**
brother, brothers	**aka, akau dodar (akau uka)**
sister, sisters	**apa, apau khokhar**
siblings (brother and sister)	**akau apa**
Your brother's name is Firuz, right?	**Nomi akai shumo Firuz ne mi?**

Note: This sentence reads literally, "Name-of brother-of you Firuz not question-particle"

Yes, you're right.	**Bale.**
uncle	**amak** (father's brother), **tagho** (mother's brother), **auntama** (father's sister), **khola** (mother's sister)
uncles	**amaku tagho**
aunts	**amau khola**
cousin (male)	**amabacha** (father's sister's son), **kholabacha** (mother's sister's son)
cousin (female)	**amadukhtar** (father's sister's daughter), **kholadukhtar** (mother's sister's daughter)
cousins	**pisar va dukhtari amau khola** (sons and daughters of father's and mother's sisters)
Where do your cousins live?	**Kholabachahoi shumo dar kujo istiqomat mekunand?**
My cousin is studying English.	**Kholabachai man zaboni anglisiro meomuzad.**
My girl-cousin is an engineer.	**Kholadukhtari man muhandis ast.**
grandchild, grandchildren	**nabera, naberaho**
His grandchild is ill.	**Naberai vay kasal ast.**

husband, wife; spouses	**shavhar, zan; zanu shavhar**
relative, relatives	**khesh, kheshu tabor**
His wife's name is Tahmina.	**Zani vay Tahmina nom dorad.**
Her husband works in the city.	**Shavhari vay dar shahr kor mekunad.**
father-/mother-in-law	**qudo**
son-in-law, daughter-in-law	**domod, kelin**
My son-in-law is a teacher.	**Domodi man muallim ast.**
Our daughter-in-law speaks Tajik well.	**Kelini mo zaboni tojikiro naghz medonad.**

ROOMS IN THE HOUSE AND FURNITURE

Utoqho va Meblho

Come visit us this evening.	**Marhamat, begoh khona biyoed.**
Gladly! Where do you live?	**Bo dilu jon! Shumo dar kujo istiqomat mekuned?**
We live in District 61, house number 43, apartment 35.	**Mo dar mikrorayoni 61-um istiqomat mekunem, khonai 43, manzili 35.**
Wow, what a nice house!	**Hoy, chi khel khonai zebo!**
Our house is old, but strong.	**Khonai mo kuhna, ammo khele mustahkam meboshad.**

How many rooms do you have?	**Manzilaton chand khona dorad?**
We have six rooms, plus a bathroom and kitchen.	**Manzilamon shashto khona, khojat-khonayu oshkhona dorad.**
This is the living room.	**In mehmonkhona meboshad.**
The living room is big.	**Mehmonkhona kalon ast.**
In the living room there are a sofa and two armchairs.	**Dar mehmonkhona yak divanu du kursi hastand.**
There are also bookshelves and a television set.	**Yak chand tochtachahoi kitob va televizor ham hastand.**
The walls are white.	**Devorho safedand.**
The ceiling is also white.	**Shift ham safed ast.**
On the floor there's a beautiful carpet.	**Dar boloi farsh qolini (gilemi) zebo meboshad.**
From the two windows our garden can be seen.	**Az du tireza boghamon namoyon ast.**
Through that door is the dining room.	**In dar ba khonai khurokkhuri mebarad.**
In the dining room there is a long table with eight chairs.	**Dar khurokkhuri mizi darozu hashto kursi hastand.**
The dining room is bright.	**Khurokkhuri khele ravshan ast.**
Where is the kitchen?	**Oshkhona dar kujo ast?**
There, next to the dining room.	**Dar peshi khurokkhuri.**

In the kitchen there is a range with an oven.	**Dar oshkhona plita (mangal) bo dukhovka (tanur) ast.**
And the refrigerator is new.	**Yakhdoni nav ham ast.**
Next to the refrigerator is a cupboard.	**Dar nazdi yakhdon jevoni khurokho ham ast.**
At the top of the stairs there are four bedrooms.	**Dar bolo chorta khobkhona ast.**
A bed and a clothes closet are in each bedroom.	**Dar khobkhonaho katu jevoni libosho hastand.**
The toilet is also upstairs.	**Khojatkhona dar bolo ham ast.**
Next to the toilet is the bathroom.	**Dar nazdi khojatkhona hammomkhona (vannakhona) ast.**
In the bathroom there are a tub and a sink.	**Dar hammomkhona vannayu dastshuyak hastand.**
We also have a shower.	**Mo dush ham dorem.**
I do not like to take baths.	**Man obboziro naghz namebinam.**
I prefer a shower.	**Man dushro naghz mebinam.**
Would you like to wash up?	**Shumo dastu ruyatonro shustan mekhohed mi?**
Yes. Where shall I wash up?	**Bale, dar kujo metavonam?**
In the bathroom, my friend!	**Dar vannakhona, dustam.**
Here's a towel for you.	**Ana sachoq baroi shumo.**

When you return, we'll eat something.	**Vaqti ki barmegarded, mo yagon chiz mekhurem.**
Where is your car?	**Moshini shumo dar kujo ast?**
The car is in the garage.	**Moshin dar garaj (iqomatgoh) ast.**
Your house is very beautiful and comfortable.	**Haqiqatan khonai shumo khele zeboyu barohat ast.**

VEHICLES

Vositahoi naqliyot

automobile/car; cars	**moshin (avtomovil), moshinho**
bus, busses	**avtobus, avtobusho**
truck, trucks	**moshini borkash, moshinahoi borkash**
airplane, airplanes	**tayora, tayoraho**
ambulance	**moshini yorii ta'jili**
bicycle, bicycle	**velosiped, velosipedho**
boat, boats	**qaiq, qaiqho**
cart, carts	**arobai ducharkha, arobahoi ducharkha**
scooter	**motoroller**
motorcycle, motorcycles	**motosikl, motosiklho**
sailboat	**kishtii bodbondor**
ship, ships	**kishti, kishtiho**
submarine	**kishtii zeriobi**
sleigh	**chana / chigina**

taxi	**taksi**
train	**poizd / qator**

COMMON OBJECTS

Obyekt(ho)i umumi

Note: To form the plural of these words, simply add the suffix *-ho*.

an atlas	**atlas**
backsack, backpack	**borkhalta**
bag, sack	**khalta / juvol / linga**
basket	**dungi**
bottle	**shisha**
book	**kitob**
broom	**jorub**
bucket	**satil**
candle	**sham**
(bank) check	**cheki bank** (pl.: **chekhoi bank**)
traveler's check	**cheki sayru sayohat**
corkscrew	**pukkashak**
dictionary	**lughat**
I'd like to buy a Tajik-English dictonary.	**Man lughati Tojiki-Anglisiro kharidan mekhoham.**
Do you have a Tajik-English dictionary?	**Oyo, shumo lughati Tojoki-Anglisiro dored mi?**
doll	**lukhtak**
a drop	**chaqra**
elevator	**lift**

envelope	**konvert**
fire	**otash**
fireplace	**otashdon**
floor	**farsh**
(drinking) glass	**stakon**
(eye) glasses	**aynak**
glue	**yelim**
grammar	**gramatika**
hammer	**bolgha**
key	**kalid**
Oh no, I've lost the key to my room!	**Sad afsus, kalidi khonaamro gum kardam!**

Note: Khona-am-ro is composed of *khona*, "house, dwelling, room," *-am*, "my," and *-ro* the specific object suffix.

It's not serious, sir. We have another key.	**Gham nakhured, janob. Mo kalidi digar dorem.**
lamp	**charogh**
letter (to mail)	**maktub**
letter (of alphabet)	**harf**
a light	**nur**
a lock	**qulf**
magazine	**majala**
map	**kharita**
matches	**gugirdho**
net	**shabaka**
WWW (world-wide web)	**shabakai tamomi jahon**
newspaper	**ruznoma**

COMMON OBJECTS

notebook	**daftar**
package	**paket / koghazpech**
passport	**pasport**
pen	**ruchka / pero**
pencil	**qalam**
penknife	**kordchai qalamtaroshi**
(straight) pin	**suzanak**
postcard	**maktubi kushoda**
radio	**aparati radio**
razor	**rishtaroshak**
electric shaver	**rishtaroshaki elektriki**
record player	**savhamonak**
road (main highway)	**shosse**
road	**roh** (pl.: **rohho**)
rope	**band**
ruler	**jadval**
scissors	**qaichi**
screwdriver	**murvattobak**
string	**bandak / resmon**
suitcase	**jomadon**
telephone	**telefon**
television set	**televizor / jahonnamo**
to watch TV	**televizor tamosho kardan**
trash can	**akhlotkutti**
tree	**darakht**
umbrella	**chatr**
visa	**viza**
window	**tireza**
wrist watch	**soati dasti** (pl.: **soathoi dasti**)

CLOTHING

Pushok-ho / Libos-ho

man's clothing	**pushokhoi mardona**
woman's clothing	**pushokhoi zanona**
belt	**tasma**
blouse	**bluzka / kurtai nimtanai zanona**
The blue blouse is pretty.	**Bluzkai kabud khele zebo ast.**
boot	**kalushi soqdor**
Whose boots are these?	**Vay kalushi soqdor az oni ki ast?**
cap	**telpak / furayhka**
coat	**kamzul / palto / plash**
dress	**kurtai zanona**
an elegant red dress	**kurtai khushdukhti surkh**
glove	**dastak**
I bought a pair of gloves.	**Man yak juft dastak kharidam.**
handkerchief	**rumolcha**
I need a white handkerchief.	**Ba man rumolchai safed lozim ast.**
hat	**kuloh**
In the winter a hat is necessary.	**Dar zamiston kuloh lozim ast.**
pants	**shim**
jeans, blue jeans	**jins, jinsi kabud**
raincoat	**abo**
scarf	**rumoli gardanpech**

I would like a silk scarf for my wife.	**Man baroi hamsaram rumoli shohii gardanpechro mekhoham.**
shirt	**kurtai tag**
How much does that white shirt cost, please?	**Iltimos, narkhi vay kurtai tag chiqadar ast?**
shoe, shoes	**poyafzol, poyafzolho**
a pair of shoes	**yak juft poyafzol**
skirt	**yubka**
socks	**jurob / paypoq**
sportcoat	**kamzuli varzish**
stockings	**jurob**
tie	**galstuk**
vest	**kamzulcha**

Traditional Tajiki Clothing:

joma	a loose-fitting garment for the upper torso

There are many kinds of **joma**, *for various seasons and holidays, for men and women. Some are colored (red, green, pink, gray), others are white or black. No traditonal outfit is complete without the* **joma**. *Since the* **joma** *does not have buttons, it needs a waist-sash to complete it:*

miyonband	cloth waist-sash
miyonbandi shohi	silk waist-sash
miyonbandi rangin	a many-colored waist-sash

In villages, women and men wear the *shalvor* and *ezor*.	**Dar qishloq zanu mard shalvoru ezor mepushand.**

shalvor	wide-legged pants
ezor	underpants

The **toqi** *is a traditional headcovering that is round or square, colored or white, simple or ornamented, for everyday use or holidays. It is worn by both women and men.*

toqi	traditional hat
sala	turban

Your turban is quite beautiful.	**Salai shumo khele zebo ast.**
City-people rarely wear turbans.	**Aholii shahr salaro khele kam mepushand.**

ANIMALS
Hayvonot

animal	**hayvon**
bird	**paranda**
hen	**murgh**
This hen lays many eggs.	**In murgh tukhmi bisyor mezoyad.**
rooster	**khurus**
With its crowing in the morning, this rooster wakes the neighbors.	**Bo ovozi subhash in khurus hamai hamsoyaro bedor mekunad.**
turkey	**hurusi murghi marjon**
Does this bird exist in your land?	**Oyo in paranda dar mamlakati shumo vujud dorad?**

Yes, but only as a domesticated bird.	**Bale, ammo parandai khonagi ast.**
drake (male duck), duck	**murghobii nar, murghobi**
The duck is going to the lake with her ducklings.	**Murghobi bo chujahoyash ba kul rafta istodaast.**
goose	**qoz**
hawk	**zaghan**
owl	**bum**
swan	**qu**
mammal	**hayvoni shirkhur**
bats	**kurshabparak**
One often sees bats after sunset.	**Kas kurshabparakro ba'd az ghurubi oftob zud-zud mebinad.**
bear	**khirs**
bull	**buqa / barzagov**
calf	**tayloq**
cat	**gurba / pishak**
cow	**gov**
dog	**sag**
My brother has three fine hunting dogs.	**Akai man se sagi zeboi shikori dorad.**
elephant	**fil**
fox	**ruboh**
goat, nanny-goat	**taka, buz**
horse	**asp**
lion	**babr**
monkey	**maymun**
They say a monkey is the fingers of the devil.	**Meguyand ki maymun angushti shayton ast.**
mouse	**mush**

I'm afraid that there are many mice in the house. — **Man metarsam, ki dar khona mush bisyor hast.**

rabbit — **khargysh**

wolves — **gurg**

Are there still wolves in the forest? — **Dar jangal boz gurg hast mi?**

fish — **mohi**

Note: There are many kinds of fishes in the streams of Tajikistan.

trout — **gulmohi**

bream — **simmohi**

catfish — **laqqamohi**

insect — **hasharot**

ant — **murcha**

Look! Many ants are marching among the trees. — **Nigoh kun! Murchahoi bisyore dar bayni darakhtho guzashta istodaand.**

butterfly — **shaparak**

fly — **pasha**

Yuck! Ugly black flies are everywhere! — **E, voye, dar dar hamma jo pashahoi la'nati!**

locust — **malakh**

mosquito — **khomushak / kurpasha**

Are there mosquitoes in Tajikistan? — **Oyo dar Tojikiston khomushak hast mi?**

Yes, there are many in damp places. — **Bale, dar joyhoi namnok khele bisyorand.**

roach — **nonkhurak**

I think that there are more roaches than stars!	**Ba fikram miqdori nonkhurakho az shumorai sitorahoi osmon ziyodand!**
spider	**tortanak**
When I see a web, I look for the spider.	**Agar tori tortanakro binam, tortanakro mekovam.**
reptile	**khazanda**
snake	**mor**
What kinds of snakes live in Tajikistan?	**Kadom morho dar Tojikiston vujud dorand?**
turtle	**sangpusht**
amphibian	**amfibia**
frog	**qurboqqa**

THE BODY

Badan

parts of the body	**qismhoi badan**
ankle	**bujulaki po**
Ow! My ankle is twisted.	**E, voy, bujulaki poyam baromad.**
arm, arms	**dast, dastho**
right arm, left arm	**dasti rost, dasti chap**
ear, ears	**gush, gushho**
A cat has two ears.	**Gurba du gush dorad.**
elbow	**orinj**
eye, the two eyes	**chashm, du chashm**
brown eyes	**chashmhoi kahvarang**
eyebrows	**qoshho**

foot, feet	**po (poy), poyho**
His right foot hurts.	**Poi rosti vay dard mekunad.**
hand, the two hands	**panjai dast, du panjai dast**
right hand, left hand	**panjai dasti rost, panjai dasti chap**
Friend, give me your hand.	**Dustam, panjai dastatro ba man te.**
knee	**zonu**
What happened to your knee?	**Ba zonuaton chi shud?**
It is swollen.	**In qadar varam kard.**
leg, legs	**soqi po, soqhoi po**
How many legs does an ant have?	**Murcha chanto po dorad?**
shoulder	**kift**
wrist	**bandi dast**
abdomen	**shikam**
back	**pusht**
beak	**nul**
This bird has a yellow beak.	**In paranda nuli zard dorad.**
beard	**rish**
My father has a long black beard.	**Padari man rishi siyohi daroz dorad.**
body	**badan**
bone	**ustukhon**
skeleton	**ustukhonband**
A skeleton is made of bones.	**Ustukhonbandi az ustukhon sokhta ast.**
brain	**maghzi sar**
chest	**sina**

chin	**manah**
eyelash	**miyha**
eyelid	**pilki chashm**
face	**ru, ruy**
I know your face, but I forget your name.	**Rui shumo shinosbarin, ammo nomatonro faromush kardam.**
finger	**angusht**
Each hand has five fingers.	**Har panjai dast panjto angusht dorad.**
fist	**musht**
If you want peace, don't shake your fist.	**Agar sulh hohed mushtro nishon nadihed.**
a hair, hair	**muy, mui sokhta**
head	**sar**
kidney	**gurda**
liver	**jigar**
mustache	**mui lab / burut**
mouth	**dahon**
The most pleasant mouth opens rarely.	**Dahoni zebotarin kam kushoda meshavad.**
nail, fingernail, toenail	**nokhun, nokhuni dast, nokhuni po**
nose	**bini**
If her nose had been a little shorter, she would have ruled the world. [said of Cleopatra]	**Agar biniash kutohtar mebud, tamomi dunyoro az khud mekard. [dar boroi Kleopatra]**
The nose is above the mouth.	**Bini dar boloi dahon ast.**
cheek	**rukhsora**
rib	**qaburgha**

skin	**pust**
stomach	**me'da**
tail	**dum**
thumb	**narangusht**
toe	**angushti po**
tongue	**zabon**
tooth	**dandon**
pain, illness	**dard, kasali**
My tooth hurts.	**Dandonam dard mekunad.**
She has a headache.	**Vay dardi sar dorad.**
He has a stomachache.	**Vay dardi me'da dorad.**
Do you have a headache?	**Oyo shumo dardi sar dored mi?**
No, my head doesn't hurt.	**Ne, saram dard namekunad.**
Is he ill?	**Oyo, vay kasal ast mi?**
Yes, a little, I think.	**Ha, kame khavotir hastam.**
What's wrong with them?	**Onhoro chi balo zad?**
Nothing. They're a bit ill.	**Hech chiz. Onho kame kasal shudaand.**
the flu	**grip**
to have a cold	**shamol khurdani**
Do you have a cold?	**Oyo shumo shamol khurded mi?**
head cold	**zukomi sar / zukomi maghzi sar**
I have a head cold.	**Saram zukom shud.**
fever	**varaja**
Do I have a fever, Doctor?	**Dukhtur, oyo man giriftori varaja shudam?**

Yes, you have a fever, but not a high one.	**Ha, shumo giriftori varaja shuded, ammo na on qadar sakht.**

COLORS
Rang-ho

color	**rang**
monochrome, one-colored	**yakranga**
multicolored	**bisyorranga / rangorang**
light colored	**ravshan**
dark	**torik**
pale	**rangparida**
blue	**kabud**
The sky is blue.	**Osmon kabud ast.**
green	**sabz**
The mountains are green.	**Kuhho sabzrang hastand.**
The house is green.	**Khona sabzrang ast.**
brown	**kahvarang** (***kahva***, "coffee")
gray	**khokistarang**
orange colored	**noranjrang**
pink (rose-colored)	**rangi gulobi**
purple	**rangi arghuvoni**
red	**surkh**
red-haired	**mallamuy**
reddish	**surkhtob**
white	**safed**
yellow	**zard**
silver	**nuqragi**

golden	**tiloi**
blond	**malla**
black	**siyoh**

PEOPLE AND PLACES
Kas(ho) va joy(ho)

man, men	**mard, mardho**
woman, women	**zan, zanho**
a person, people	**kas, kas-ho**
child, children	**kudak, kudak-ho**
boy, boys	**bacha, bachaho**
girl, girls	**dukhtar, dukhtarho**
appartment	**manzil**
baker	**nonpaz** (*non*, "bread")
bakery	**nonpazkhona** (*khona*, "house")
Where is the bakery, please?	**Iltimos, nonpazkhona dar kujo ast?**
Over there, next to the pharmacy.	**Dar onjo, dar nazdi dorukhona.**
bank	**bank**
banker	**bankir**
beauty shop	**oroishkhona**
imam (religious leader)	**emom**
bookstore	**dukoni kitob**
Is there a bookstore nearby?	**Oyo, dar atrofi nazdik dukoni kitob ast mi?**
bread shop	**dukoni non**
When does the bread shop open?	**Dukoni non kay kushoda meshavad?**

butcher	**qassob**
butcher shop	**dukoni gusht**
Hurry! The butcher shop is going to close soon.	**Chaqon bosh! Dukoni gusht khozir makhkam meshavad.**
café	**kahvakhona** (LIT: "coffee house")
I like the cafés of Paris.	**Kahvakhonahoi Paris ba man khele mahqul hastand.**
castle	**qal'a**
cemetary	**qabriston**
In this cemetary there is the tomb of a holy man.	**Dar in qabriston qabri avliyo mavjud ast.**
cinema, movie theater	**sinamo, kinoteatr**
You know what, let's go to the cinema this evening.	**Gush kun, biyo in begoh ba sinamo meravem.**
What kind of film will we see?	**Kadom filmro tamosho mekunem?**
It doesn't matter.	**Ahamiyat nadorad**
city	**shahr**
city hall	**hukumati shahr**
city person	**shahrvand**
in center-city, downtown	**dar markazi shahr**
small city	**shahrcha**
customs	**gumruk**
customs officer	**gumrukchi**
dentist	**dandonsoz**
doctor, physician	**tabib**
I need a doctor who understands English.	**Ba man tabibe lozim ast, ki zaboni anglisirofahmad.**

embassy	**saforatkhona**
factory	**korkhona** (*kor*, "work"), **zavod**
Before independence, many workers worked in that factory.	**Pesh az istiqlol korgaroni bisyor dar in zavod kor mekardand.**
farm	**ferma**
farmer, cultivator	**kishtgardonchi, zaminkor**
For farmers, cotton is a very important crop.	**Baroi zaminkoron ziroati pakhta khele muhim ast.**
fish market	**dukoni mohi**
fisherman	**mohigir**
This weekend, let's go to the mountains to fish.	**Biyoed dar okhiri hafta baroi mohigiri ba kuhiston ravem.**
(art) gallery	**namoishgoh**
garage (at home)	**iqomatgoh**
garage (for repairs)	**garajh**
garden	**bogh**
In the courtyard of this house there is a beautiful garden.	**Dar nazdi vay khona boghi zebo ast.**
grocery store, food store	**maghozai khurokvori**
In winter, the food stores don't have a great variety of foodstuffs.	**Dar zamiston khurokvoriho nav'i khurokhoi gunogun nadorand.**
guide	**rohbar**

Note: Don't be frightened by the sound of this word: it may sound a bit like "robber" to English-speakers!

PEOPLE AND PLACES

Where can I find a guide who speaks English?	**Rohbare, ki ba zaboni anglisi harf mezanad, az kujo yoftan mumkin ast?**
Many guides speak Russian.	**Aqsariyati rohbarho ba zaboni rusi harf mezanand.**
hospital	**kasalkhona, tabobatkhona**
hotel	**mehmonkhona**
hotelkeeper	**mehmonkhonachi**
house	**khona**
at home	**dar nazdi khona**
laundry	**joi libosshui**
library	**kitobkhona** ("book house")
lighthouse	**mino**
market place	**bozor**
mayor	**raisi hukumati shahr**
mayor's office	**hukumati shahr**
Is the mayor working today?	**Oyo, raisi hukumati shahr imruz kor mekunad mi?**
merchant	**tijoratchi, savdogar mosque masjid**
museum	**muzey**
Which museum is that one over there?	**Dar onjo chi khel muzey ast?**
palace	**qasr**
pharmacist	**dorusoz**
pharmacy	**dorukhona**
I will become a pharmacist.	**Man dorusoz/farmazeft meshavam.**
the policc	**polis**

police officer	**polischi**
police station	**poliskhona**
postman	**korgari shu'bai aloqa**
post office	**shu'bai aloqa**
professor	**profesor**
restaurant	**restoran**
Please suggest to me a very good restaurant.	**Iltimos, yagon restorani khubro ba man guyed.**
I know a very good one, but it is also very expensive.	**Khele khubro medonam, ammo khele qimat ast.**
school	**maktab**
Where is the school in your city?	**Dar shahri shumo maktab dar kujo ast?**
public square	**maydon**
station	**vokzal**

Note: Here is another word which has become a world-traveler. The Russians borrowed their word for "railroad station" from the British "Vauxhall" station. Of course, the Russians spelled "Vauxhall" as it sounded to them, *vokzal*. The Tajiks then borrowed the Russian word.

I am looking for the train station.	**Man vokzalro justuju mekunam.**
store	**maghoza, dukon**
department store	**majala**
tavern, bar	**maykhona, bar**
teacher (male)	**muallim**
teacher (female)	**muallima**
My father is a teacher.	**Padari man muallim ast.**
watchmaker	**soatsoz**
watchmaker's store	**ustokhonai soatsoz**

worker (male)	**korgar**
worker (female)	**korgarzan**
work place	**korkhona**
yard	**havli**
During the holidays, there are a lot of tourists.	**Dar ruzhoi istirohat sayohatchiyon bisyor meshavand.**

HAVE TO, WANT TO, BE ABLE TO
Majbur shudan, Hohish doshtan, Tavoniatan

obligation, duty	**majburi, vazifa**
prohibition	**ma'nkuni**
knowledge	**donish**
capability	**qobiliyat**
pleasure	**ma'qul, khush**
displeasure	**noma'qul, nokhush**
wish, desire	**iroda, khohish**
willingly	**bo dilu jon**
to like	**naghz didan**
I like to play tennis.	**Man tenisboziro naghz mebinam.**
soccer	**futbol**
Do you like to watch soccer games?	**Tamoshoi musobiqai futbolbozonro shumo naghz mebined mi?**
Yes! I like to watch soccer a lot.	**Bale! Futbolboziro khele naghz mebinam.**
My friends don't like soccer.	**Dusthoi man futbolro naghz namebinand.**
to be pleasing to	**foridan ba**

I like tennis.	**Tenisbozi ba man meforad.**
I don't like tennis.	**Tenisbozi ba man nameforad.**
to prefer	**behtar donistan/ shumurdan**
I prefer soccer to tennis.	**Man futbolboziro nisbat ba tenisbozi behtar meshumuram.**
to want, to desire	**khostan, talabidan**
I want to learn Tajik.	**Mekhoham zaboni tojikiro omuzam.**
I don't want to play tennis.	**Man tenisbozi kardan namekhoham.**
I don't want to forget that.	**Man inro faromush kardan namekhoham.**
to be obligated to	**maghbur shudan**
I have to leave now.	**Khozir man majbur hastam ravam.**
I must telephone my company.	**Man boyad ba shirkatamon telefon kunam.**
You should speak to your friend.	**Shumo boyad ba dustaton suhan gued.**
You must speak with your friend.	**Khele lozim ast, ki shumo ba dustaton suhan gued.**
Can you understand me?	**Shumo maro fahmidan metavoned mi?**
Can you swim?	**Shumo obbozi kardan metavoned mi?**
It is forbidden for you to smoke here.	**Ruhsat nest, ki shumo dar injo sigor choked.**
Don't do that!	**Inro nakuned!**

SOME IMPORTANT SIGNS

Yakchand e'lonho va varaqhoijalbkunanda

Entrance	**Daromadgoh**
Exit	**Baromadgoh**
(Bus) Stop	**Istgoh(i avtobus)**
Warning!	**Diqqat!**
Warning! This water is not drinkable!	**Diqqat! In obi nushoki nest!**
Swimming Forbidden	**Obbozi kardan ma'n ast**
Please do not smoke.	**Iltimos, sigor nachoked**
Smoking Forbidden	**Sigor chokidan ma'n ast**
Danger!	**Khatarnok!**
Silence!	**Homush bosh!**
Parking	**Joi moshin moni**
No Parking!	**Dar in jo moshinro namoned!**
Warning! Road Closed!	**Diqqat! Roh basta ast!**
Police	**Polis**
Hospital	**Tabobatkhona**
Train Station	**Vokzal**
Taxi stand	**Istgohi taksi**
Tourist office	**Shirkati sayohati**

SOME PROVERBS AND SAYINGS

Zarbulmasalu maqol

One way of getting an insight into the thinking of a people is to look at common sayings and proverbs. Here are a few from Tajikistan:

Naburdani ranj - nomuyassari ganj.

No treasure is gotten without work.

Bo yak gul bahor nameshavad.

Spring is not made from one flower.

Garchi tillo khurdast, qimmqtash buzurg ast.

A small bird may have sharp claws.

Gul khor doradu, asal - oru.

A flower has thorns; honey, bees.

Durugh furugh nadorad.

A lie does not have good consequences.

Sukut alomati rizo ast.

Silence is a sign of consent.

Az gunjishk tarsi, arzan nakor.

If you fear sparrows, don't sow millet.

Non dar nondonu, kalidash dar osmon.

The bread is in the basket; the key, in heaven.

Ba labi ob burda tashna ovardan.

To bring a thirsty person to the bank of a river.

Zurii behuda miyon meshikanad.

A vain attempt breaks the back.

TALKING ABOUT TAJIKISTAN AND THE TAJIKS

The word *tojik* comes from the word *tojdor*, "having a crown." This derives from *toj*, "a crown." In ancient times, Tajiks wore a small crown on their heads to distinguish themselves from neighboring groups. This same crown now appears on the flag and coat of arms of the Tajik Republic.

The national flag of Tajikistan is a rectangle consisting of three horizontal bands. The top band is red; the bottom, green. The middle band is white and equal to one-and-a-half the width of the other bands. On this white band, in the middle, there is a golden crown topped by a semi-circle of seven stars. The ratio of width to length of this flag is 1:2.

Tajik (ethnic name)	**tojik**
Tajikistan	**Tojikiston**
Tajik (adjective)	**tojiki**
Tajik clothing	**libosi tojiki**
Tajik language	**tojiki**
President	**prezident, rais**
President of the Republic	**prezidenti/ raisi jumkhur**
(government) minister	**vazir**
meeting, assembly	**majlis**

TAJIK ON THE INTERNET

There are several sites on the Internet with information about Tajikistan and the Tajiks. To pursue your own interests, we recommend using your favorite browser with the requests "Tajik, Tajiki, Tajik language or Tajikistan." This should get you started.

The University of Minnesota has a Central Asian Studies Program, and two excellent sites originate there, both prepared by Professor Bashiri. At **http://www.ilasll.umn.edu/bashiri/Masov's%20History/summary.html** you will find background information on events in Tajikistan just prior to and in the years since the breakup of the Soviet Union. At **http://www. ilasll.umn.edu/bashiri/Tajling%20folder/Tajling.html** there is information about ethnic and linguistic divisions in Tajikistan.

A wealth of information about Tajikistan is also available at **http://www.wlc.com/oxus/centasia.htm**. Once you reach this site, select *Tajikistan*, and you will find links to many other sites.

If you are interested in listening to Tajik-language broadcasts on the radio, **http://www. rferl. org/BD/TA/ta-schedule.html** has current listings of broadcast schedules.

For a personal view of life in Dushanbe, Alex Kondur's web page is interesting. You can reach it at **http://comdinet.com/tn/alex.htm**.

Finally, if you think you might like to take a summer course in Tajik, check the information at **http://www.actr.org/**, a listing of programs throughout the Russian-speaking world which includes non-Russian cultures of the former Soviet Union. The University of Minnesota, Central Asian Studies Department, also has information on courses. The University of Washington, in the state of Washington, has courses as well.

USEFUL CONTACTS AND ADDRESSES

If you are interested in doing business in Tajikistan, or just want to visit, the following addresses will be useful.

U.S Embassy - Dushanbe
Ambassador - R. Grant Smith
Hotel October
4th Floor
105A Rudaki Street
734025 Dushanbe, Republic of Tajikistan
telephone: 7-3772-21-03-56
fax: 7-3772-21-03-62

You can also contact the State Department for information about conditions in Tajikistan, or for any possible advisories to travelers.

Business Initiative Center
Suite 300
40 Rudaki Street
Dushanbe, Tajikistan 743000
telephone: 7-3772-21-05-28

Tajikistan does not yet have an embassy in Washington. For information about the country, you can contact the Tajikistan Mission to the United Nations:

Ambassador - Rashid Alimov
136 East 67th Street
New York, NY 10021
telephone: (212) 744-2196
fax: (212) 472-7645

BIBLIOGRAPHY

Benson, P. *Comprehensive English-Esperanto Dictionary*. El Cerrito, CA: Esperanto League for North America, 1995.

Comrie, B. *The World's Major Languages*. Oxford, UK: Oxford University Press, 1990.

Conroy, J.F. *Breton Dictionary and Phrasebook*. New York: Hippocrene, 1997.

Lambton, A.K.S. *Persian Grammar*. Cambridge, UK: Cambridge University Press, 1974.

Lazard, G. "Persian and Tajik." In T. Sebeok, ed., *Current Trends in Linguistics*, Vol. 6: 64-96. Paris: Mouten, 19702

MAP

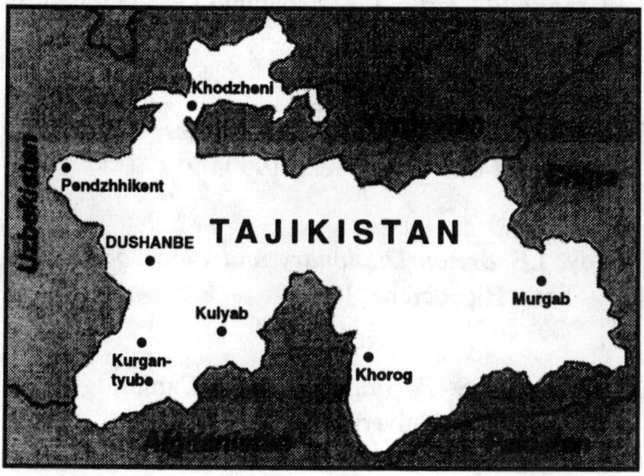
Khodzheni
Pendzhhikent
TAJIKISTAN
DUSHANBE
Kulyab
Murgab
Kurgan-
tyube
Khorog

LITHUANIAN-ENGLISH/ENGLISH LITHUANIAN CONCISE DICTIONARY
382 pp • 4 x 6 • 10,000 entries • 0-7818-0151-6 • W • $14.95pb • (489)

LITHUANIAN-ENGLISH/ENGLISH LITHUANIAN COMPACT DICTIONARY
400 pp • 3½ x 4 ¾ • 10,000 entries • 0-7818-0536-8 • W • $8.95pb • (624)

RUSSIAN-ENGLISH COMPREHENSIVE DICTIONARY
Oleg Benyukh, General Editor
800 pp • 6 x 9 • 0-7818-0506-6 • W • $60.00hc • (612)

ENGLISH-RUSSIAN COMPREHENSIVE DICTIONARY
800 pp • 8 ½ x 11 • 50,000 entries • 0-7818-0353-5 • W • $60.00hc • (312)0-7818-0442-6 • W • $35.00pb • (50)

RUSSIAN-ENGLISH/ENGLISH-RUSSIAN STANDARD DICTIONARY, Revised Edition With Business Terms
418 pp • 5 ½ x 8 ½ • 32,000 entries • 0-7818-0280-6 • W • $18.95pb • (322)

ENGLISH-RUSSIAN STANDARD DICTIONARY
214 pp • 5 ½ x 8 ½ • 16,000 entries • 0-87052-100-4 • W • $11.95pb • (239)

RUSSIAN-ENGLISH/ENGLISH-RUSSIAN CONCISE DICTIONARY
536 pp • 4 ½ x 6 10,000 entries • 0-7818-0132-X • W • $11.95pb (262)

RUSSIAN-ENGLISH/ENGLISH-RUSSIAN COMPACT DICTIONARY
536 pp 3 1/8 x 4 5/8 10,000 entries 0-7818-0537-6 W $9.95pb • (688)

RUSSIAN HANDY DICTIONARY
120 pp • 5 x 7 ¾ • 0-7818-0013-7 USA • $8.95pb • (371)